THE MAN-EATING MYTH

Gary

Olson

THE
MAN-EATING MYTH
ANTHROPOLOGY & ANTHROPOPHAGY

W. Arens

OXFORD UNIVERSITY PRESS

Oxford   New York   Toronto   Melbourne

Oxford University Press
Oxford London Glasgow
New York Toronto Melbourne Wellington
Nairobi Dar es Salaam Cape Town
Kuala Lumpur Singapore Jakarta Hong Kong Tokyo
Delhi Bombay Calcutta Madras Karachi

Copyright © 1979 by Oxford University Press, Inc.
First published by Oxford University Press, New York, 1979
First issued as an Oxford University Press paperback, 1980

Library of Congress Cataloging in Publication Data

Arens, W   1940-
  The man-eating myth.

  Bibliography: p.
  Includes index.
  1. Cannibalism. I. Title.
GN409.A73   394'.9   78-23387
ISBN 0-19-502506-7
ISBN 0-19-502793-0 pbk.

Printed in the United States of America

PREFACE

My interest in man-eaters was sparked innocently enough. A student in an introductory course I was teaching asked at mid-semester why I was lecturing on kinship, politics and economics instead of more interesting things like witchcraft, fieldwork experiences and cannibalism. This comment struck a sympathetic chord, since I remembered that these were very much like the topics which attracted me to my first anthropology course as an undergraduate. If I remember correctly, my instructor did not pay much attention to these matters, either. Even though I continued on in anthropology, these initial interests faded as I devoted more attention to the esoteric than the exotic. This trend was natural enough for a professional academic, but I did not see why first-year university students should have to suffer for it. Consequently, in preparing for a lecture, I turned to the study of man-eaters, which was eventually transformed into this study of the myth of man-eating. I mention this to make it clear to readers that, like themselves, when I began to think about the subject I was already of the opinion that cannibalism in the past and present was a fairly common phenomenon. The essay which follows is the result of a conversion process.

Like many other significant experiences in life, the task was pleasant to anticipate and worth having done. However, the intervening stage was another matter entirely. Among other things, I learned why writers think the pen is mightier than the sword. Very often it is heavier, and at times almost impossible to heft with any grace. I also became depressingly aware that when not discussing some safely narrow topic such as ethnicity in contemporary rural Tanzania, about which for obvious reasons the author may immediately be among the world's foremost authorities, there are almost insurmountable qualitative and quantitative difficulties to overcome. As a result, writing has paradoxically been a lonely occupation requiring the assistance of many others. For example, I can recall talking to an orientalist who referred me to sources which mentioned that in China it was believed Koreans were cannibals, while in Korea the opposite belief prevailed. When I mentioned how difficult it was at the time to keep track of everything and everyone, she informed me that in the East it was the felicitous Year of the Cat.

There was comfort in the omens, but often I had to turn to others for different support services. There were some who offered practical advice and assistance, others who showed faith, and finally some whose mere presence was inspirational. The book could not have been completed without all of them. They include: Diana Antos Arens, Geoffrey W. Arens, John W. Burton, Nancy Fairley, D. Carleton Gajdusek, Paula Brown Glick, Michael Gramly, Ronald Greene, David Hicks, Ivan Karp, Charles Malemud, Rodney Needham, Stanley Regelson, Lawrence J. Taylor, Robert J. Tilley, Mari Walker, John Williams, Roy Willis, and Kathy Yunger. I leave it to them to sort themselves out. All have been encouraging, but not always in total agreement, so more than academic form requires that I accept responsibility for any errors of fact or interpretation. On the other hand, there are those anonymous colleagues who have provided negative reinforcement by advising me not to stick my neck out or to concern myself with more serious scholarship. Their attitude further stimulated my curiosity, especially in the area of the anthropological investment in the idea of cannibalism.

Because of the nature of the subject and the critical tone of much of what follows, I find it difficult to dedicate this book to any single person. In general, I hope that in some way it will provide meaning for a younger generation, including those to become anthropologists, who will find no need for a world thought to be inhabited by man-eating monsters.

W.A.

Stony Brook, N.Y.
August 1978

CONTENTS

Illustrations

No discipline can hope to keep control over the popular uses of its work. But every now and then its assumptions need to be checked, not so much for the sake of the general public, who will always do what they like, but for the sake of the discipline itself.

Mary Douglas

Both Europeans and Arabs seem to have a morbid interest in cannibalism and tend to accept almost any tale told them about it.

E. E. Evans-Pritchard

THE MAN-EATING MYTH

1

THE NATURE
OF ANTHROPOLOGY
& ANTHROPOPHAGY

In a fit of optimism characteristic of the era, those few scattered intellectuals of the nineteenth century with an interest in human cultures christened their nascent discipline *anthropology*, the study of man. This definition may now seem grandiose, but it suited the grand interests of these early practitioners, who set about to create a new intellectual perspective which would investigate the universal human condition. Broad issues were clearly the order of the day, so that a systematic reconstruction of the history of mankind and the discovery of the bases of human thought and action were thought to be reasonable concerns. As one distinguished contemporary anthropologist has put it, there was at the time an immodest "craving for generality" (Needham 1972: 219).

This ambitious new calling attracted an international cast trained in the classics, history, philosophy and comparative jurisprudence who subsequently became the ancestors of modern social anthropology. Their production, in the form of massive multi-volumed works, was Herculean by present academic standards. These feats, intended for the enlightenment of their colleagues and the educated public as well, stand as fascinating testimony to a not too distant past. Nonetheless, despite the sense of commitment and intellectual ability, the task proved beyond their competence. Sterile disputes, rather than acceptable conclusions about the origin of institutions and the nature of thought, were the outcome of over fifty years of scholarship by some of the greatest minds of the age.

Although none of the once-commanding issues were successfully resolved, the twentieth-century descendants of the tradition, though they retained the original name and definition of the discipline, radically restricted its perimeters in order to focus attention on more narrowly defined problems. There are a number of explanations for this retrenchment in addition to the realization that the pioneers suffered from the delusions of intellectual grandeur which often accompany a lack of appreciation for the difficulties attending on a previously untried endeavor. These armchair theorizers' apparent lack of reliable data pointed to the need for first-hand experience with other cultures.

Instead of offering easy solutions, a stint of actual fieldwork as a method of data collection vividly demonstrated the nature of the problem. Acquiring systematic understanding of the underlying rationale of thought and behavior among an exotic group of people proved to be no mean feat; and the inability to resolve modest issues which the earlier thinkers failed to even recognize as problems signaled the end of the era of grand theory for some time to come. Instead each anthropologist became the interpreter of a particular group of people—on a far-flung island or remote interior village. The public may still occasionally demand some profound commentary on the human experience, but other professionals fail to lend any credence to such pronouncements, most often by pointing out that such a condition does not hold among "their" people. Academic professionalization assumes that meaningful communication can only take place among colleagues. To quote Needham again: "Debates can still make something of a clamour, but the issues can often appear no more worthy of general attention than were the cobwebs derided by Kant" (1973: 785). The problems which now stimulate the most interest are those of our own making, as the devotees dispute the proper interpretation of color in a single ritual or a term in a particular kinship system. Thus in a real sense the discipline feeds on its own inadequacies and inability to produce the simplest satisfactory generalizations. In less than a hundred years anthropology abandoned common concerns and broad appeal for topics now often of interest only to a few specialists with shared esoteric inclinations. Considering the complex nature of the human mind and its cultural products, probably no other outcome could be reasonably expected. This does not negate the fact that much of the excitement and optimism of an earlier era has been replaced by a contemporary sense of futility and outright cynicism on the part of many anthropologists.

This frame of mind was inevitable because one feature of minute specialization is the tendency for mechanical manipulation and calculation to replace speculation and reflection. Consequently, in comparison with other social sciences, anthropology has also been negligent in encouraging a reflexive attitude toward the discipline itself. Except for the "rethinking" of traditional problems on the part of senior scholars and the critique of the comfortable relationship between a former theoretical orientation and the then-prevailing political ideology, anthropologists have been content to let more enduring notions remain unexamined. However, re-analysis and hindsight are not always the same as reflection and self-doubt. The belief that anthropologists possess an unbiased view of human nature, based upon a personal experience with another culture and a literary acquaintance with many others, undoubtedly has much to do with this self-assurance. Eliminating ethnocentricism and replacing this subjective orientation with objective analysis is regarded as the primary aim of the anthropological inquiry. However, is this assumption about the underlying nature of the discipline always warranted? The academic record indicates that despite assurances to the contrary, scholars in all fields occasionally have functioned as little more than erudite purveyors of attractive pedestrian myths. In the case of anthropology it is impossible to view nineteenth-century theories grounded in the notions of human progress and western cultural superiority without coming to such a conclusion.

Few today would argue that social anthropology has emerged in our time as a natural science. In addition to being an academic discipline and art form, anthropology also involves the practitioners with a peculiar vision of the social universe. Anthropology can also be thought of as a secular world-view weaving together demonstrated facts with unstated assumptions about human nature. As such it contains much which is fundamental to our own historical and cultural experience. This is demonstrated by the difficulty non-western university students often experience in coming to grips with anthropology and other social sciences, although they may excel in the "hard" sciences. The simple techniques and accumulated facts are not the problem. Instead the perplexing issue for them is more likely an appreciation of the rationale for undertaking the exercise.

Admittedly, considering whether or not people actually eat human flesh and examining the commentary on this purported phenomenon will not in itself provide a completely satisfactory answer to some of the questions posed here. On the other hand, anthropophagy is one of the unchallenged "facts" of anthropology which each successive theory of human nature has attempted to interpret anew. Consequently, reviewing this material invites a confrontation with some basic anthropological assumptions about human nature which have managed to ingratiate themselves within the discipline.

The references to man eating man are so pervasive in the literature on other cultures that some popular writers (cf. Hogg 1973 and Sagan 1974) have implied the existence of a conspiracy on the part of professional anthropologists to keep the full facts and scientific explanations for such "uncivilized" behavior from the general public. A professional anthropologist has even recently lodged a similar charge in both learned and popular forums against his colleagues (Harner 1977a and 1977b). He argues that, as the result of a misguided sense of scholarly morality, students of Mesoamerican history have "covered up" the evidence on the true extent of Aztec human sacrifice and cannibalism prior to European contact. Cannibalism is so good to think about that the intellectual appetite is not easily satisfied, despite the amount of information readily available. Every encyclopedia contains a commentary on the topic by a recognized scholar, and almost every anthropologist considers it a sacred duty to report that the people studied and lived among were in the past or just recently eaters of their own kind.

In light of the preceding comments, this essay has a dual purpose. First, to assess critically the instances of and documentation for cannibalism, and second, by examining this material and the theoretical explanations offered, to arrive at some broader understanding of the nature and function of anthropology over the past century. In other words, the question of whether or not people eat each other is taken as interesting but moot. But if the idea that they do is commonly accepted without adequate documentation, then the reason for this state of affairs is an even more intriguing problem.

The reader should be forewarned of the biases or at least orientations which underlie this study. First, as the result of directed research, conversations with colleagues and some deliberation, I am dubious about the actual existence of this act as an accepted practice for any time or place. Recourse to cannibalism under survival conditions or as a rare instance of antisocial behavior is not denied for any culture. But whenever it occurs this is considered a regrettable act rather than custom. This position of course flies in the face of conventional wisdom and the numerous reports; but little of genuine interest would result from attempting to confirm the acceptable and obvious. A deeper appreciation of the world we live in is achieved by demonstrating that generally held assumptions are false or at least debatable. In the words of Montaigne, who gave some thought to cannibalism, "we are to judge by the eye of reason, and not from common report" (Montaigne 1952: 91). His advice would be even more encouraging if he had not concluded that cannibals abounded in other parts of the world, but that they could be excused because they were savages.

The second guiding assumption of this study is the belief that in examining a problem it is just as important to demonstrate how a particular idea, whether true or false, becomes part of conventional wisdom. In this regard, I propose that anthropology has not maintained the usual standards of documentation and intellectual rigor expected when other topics are being considered. Instead, it has chosen uncritically to lend its support to the collective representations and thinly disguised prejudices of western culture about others. Indeed, I find it difficult to understand how learned debates could rage for decades on whether or not a particular marriage system actually exists, while we merely assume that people have eaten and continue to eat each other. If one of the primary tasks of anthropology is to uncover what is essential or common to humanity, then the existing state of affairs is astonishing.

But let us start at the beginning. "These Scythian husband-men then occupy the country eastward, for three days' journey. . . . Beyond this region the country is desert for a great distance; and beyond the desert Androphagi dwell. . . . The Androphagi have the most savage customs of all men; they pay no regard to justice, nor make use of any established law. They are nomads, and wear a dress like a Scythian; *they speak* [author's italics] a peculiar language; and of these nations, are the only people that eat human flesh" (Herodotus 1879: 243; 272-73).

Difficult as it may be to outline systematically the development of anthropology, the task of pinpointing the origin of the cannibal notion is truly beyond possibility. Like the feud, the idea that others at some far distance eat human flesh knows no beginning and probably will know no end. However, it should be noted that Herodotus, who is often thought of as the first recorder of other cultures, felt compelled to inform his readers in the fifth century B.C. that some unknown people, far beyond the pale of civilization, resorted to this barbaric custom. Thus, perhaps not coincidentally, anthropology and the notion of anthropophagy made their literary appearance at the same time in the cradle of western civilization.

My own personal introduction to this topic can be recorded with greater precision. Shortly after I began fieldwork in a rural community in Tanzania in 1968, a resident who had gone out of

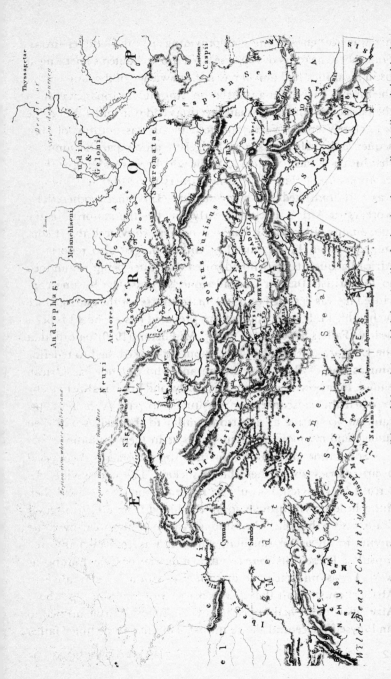

Map accompanying a nineteenth-century edition of Herodotus which locates the Androphagi according to the original text—on the fringe of known civilization in the fifth century B. C. (upper center).

his way to befriend me was providing a tour of the environs. Somewhere near his own house a neighbor shouted something at us in Swahili. I had only a passing knowledge of the language at the time so I asked for a translation, since it was apparent even to the newcomer that more than greetings had transpired. My guide was clearly embarrassed, and told me it was nothing of consequence; but after persistent badgering on my part he admitted that his co-resident wanted to know why he was walking with an *mchinja-chinja*. The obvious next query revealed that the phrase was best translated as "blood-sucker." Like many other fieldworkers in Africa, I learned early on that the majority of the inhabitants either had suspicions or were convinced that I consumed human blood. Another anthropologist also reports an African acquaintance who admitted that, after being summoned to the British District Commissioner's House, he became convinced he was destined to be the main course for the guests. Since he had his knife with him, he was prepared to surrender his body dearly (Fallers 1969: 83). Finally, Middleton (1970) reports that the Lubgara of Uganda, with whom he worked, had to redefine him as one of those rare Europeans who did not eat African babies. In my own case, I optimistically, and I now realize naively, expected this misconception eventually to pass as the residents came to accept me as a person similar to themselves and then understand my more mundane purpose in their community.

Some time later, from more trusting informants, I collected bizarre stories about these blood-suckers. The tales vividly described how a victim would be rendered unconscious and then hung head down in order to let the blood from the slit jugular drain into a bucket. The fluid was then transported by a fire engine to an urban hospital, where it was converted into red capsules. These pills were taken on a regular basis by Europeans who, I was informed, needed these potations to stay alive in Africa. I must admit that it was exactly stories of this type about Africans which I had hoped to collect, but I was disconcerted to find myself the central figure in such a drama. At the time I failed to appreciate the political symbolism of the narrative, which cast colonial Europeans as the consumers of African vitality, and paternally concluded that the Africans were entitled to their ignorance. To my dismay, many still clung to the suspicion a year and a half later at my departure. In addition, I was troubled by the tenacity of their belief in this common variation on the cannibalism theme without a shred of concrete evidence. It was true that the British had tried unsuccessfully to mount a blood drive during World War II in their former colony for the African troops fighting overseas, and there was indeed a fire engine stationed not far away at a small airstrip, even though there had never been a fire. To some Africans, this apparently constituted enough circumstantial evidence to substantiate a European conspiracy to drink African blood. Upon reflection, similar beliefs about Africans on our part no longer seemed so reasonable. A review (Harrell-Bond 1975) of a recent addition to the literature on African cannibalism, which included mention that a woman in contemporary Russia was accused of cannibalism because she was a Baptist, rekindled an interest in the problem.

I soon became aware that the cannibal epithet at one time or another has been applied by someone to every human group. A random list of the more spectacular anthropophagists gleaned from textbooks included the "Congo" of Africa, who fattened their war prisoners to the desired plumpness before serving them up; the Fijian chiefs who regularly dined on human flesh; New Guineans whose human cargo was consumed one at a time during long river voyages; the Aztecs, who participated in mass cannibalistic orgies at rituals; and the South American Tupinamba, whose culinary arts included elaborate rules of etiquette in distributing human cutlets. Considering that a primary intent of such books is to capture the students' attention, which is often related to sales, the exaggerated colorful prose is not surprising. Subsequent research also indicated there was some basis for such claims in existing publications, most often from an earlier period. It is appropriate, therefore, to pick up the cannibal trail again.

Relying on the authority of St. Jerome, Gibbon (1900) reported that the Scots and Picts of pre-Christian England formerly delighted in "the taste of human flesh" so that they attacked the shepherd rather than his flock "for their horrid repasts." The subsequent progress of the Scots, though, leads Gibbon optimistically to conclude with "the pleasing hope that New Zealand may produce, in some future age, the Hume of the Southern Hemisphere" (508–9). In a similar frame of mind, Marx and Engels early in the nineteenth century quote the ancient geographer Strabo, who wrote of the Irish: "Concerning this island I have nothing certain to tell, except that the inhabitants are more savage than the Britons, since they are man-eaters, . . . and since they count it an honorable thing, when their fathers die, to devour them" (1971: 198). He also mentions that these Irish failed to recognize the incest taboo. Such accounts are still acceptable, for they make the familiar equation between the assumed culture of our ancestors two thousand years ago and that of twentieth-century non-westerners, who were cannibals and sexually indiscriminate until recently. The above quotation is so often reproduced in this abbreviated form that the concluding phrase from the original source comes as a surprise. It adds: ". . . but I am saying this only with the understanding that I have no trustworthy witnesses for it" (Strabo 1939: 261). In addition to suggesting that the author had higher standards of ethnographic reporting than many of his latter-day imitators, the use of the truncated sentence by others exemplifies how the view we hold of our own cultural past is coerced to coincide with our contemporary image of the non-western world. Montagu's suggestion (1968: 6) that such an analogy is "pathetically calculated to provide a lift for the faltering ego" is apt.

Though the flaws in this line of reasoning are now obvious, nineteenth-century evolutionary social theory attempted to assign specific social and cultural features to corresponding eras of history. Certain institutional forms and ideas were thought to be characteristic of earlier epochs. Using this assumption, theorists

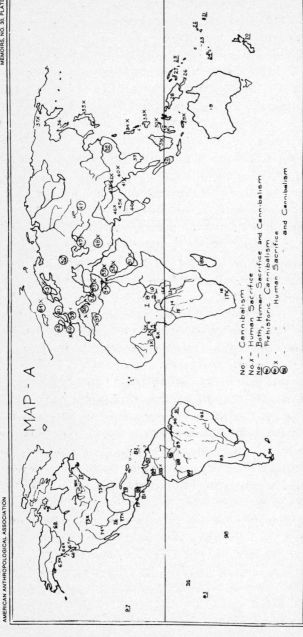

CANNABALISM AND HUMAN SACRIFICE

Illustration from Loeb's *The Blood Sacrifice Complex,* correlating presumed European prehistoric cannibal sites with early-twentieth-century man-eating areas of the non-western world.

hoped to reconstruct social development by studying and categorizing the traits of both past and present societies. The notion of cannibalism neatly fits into the picture. In this schema, prehistoric man (as evidenced from some of the bones he left behind) and certain of the most primitive contemporary groups (reports of whom indicated that they practiced cannibalism in the quest for food) were mired in the early stage. In a subsequent period characterized by the most complex non-western civilizations, human flesh was used only in religious rituals. In the western cultural annals, as in the epoch portrayed in the Old Testament, animals were substituted for humans. Finally, in the last stage, exemplified most dramatically by our present condition, the concrete act of anthropophagy has been replaced by a symbolic sacrifice and the consumption of a spiritual essence. In this historical outline, each stage reflects a more symbolic and abstract intellectual ability than its predecessor. A pioneer American anthropologist who subscribed to this evolutionary formula succinctly and graphically illustrated the perspective in a map accompanying his study *The Blood Sacrifice Complex* (Loeb 1927). The sites for European cannibalism and human sacrifice are all dated to the prehistoric eons and those for the non-European world to the present or recent period. However, such a correlation is not a valid historical analogy but merely matches a fictionalized past with a dubious present. As this inquiry will demonstrate, Loeb's portrayal may be an adequate map of the twentieth-century imagination but it leaves something to be desired as an objective historical record.

An encounter with the more contemporary professional literature turns up more circumscribed discussions as the delicate cobwebs are dutifully spun. The most recent concern is the ecological debate, complete with caloric counts of the potential nutritional value of human flesh. Predictably, there is little agreement as some (Garn and Block 1970) claim there is no nutritional sense to the practice, while others (Dornstreich and Morren 1974) argue that there is some worthwhile sustenance entailed. The following quote conveys the objective nature of present publications. "Data from different New Guinea societies indicate that the balance between different protein inputs varies with such things as ecological zonation and the structure of local ecosystems involving human populations" (Dornstreich and Morren 1974: 10). Which side of the argument this is meant to support is unclear, but the discussion is obviously meant to be "scientific."

At the other extreme are the structuralists. This camp shows little interest in the concrete implications of the act out of preference for a symbolic interpretation which will permit integration of the idea with broader cultural patterns. Thus the master of structuralism, Lévi-Strauss (1966), suggests that boiling is the usual preparation of food for domestic consumption while roasting is more typical for food to be served to guests. As an extension of this model, he proposes that among cannibals boiling will be most often employed in preparing kin, with roasting the preferred method for enemies. However, Shankman (1969) finds this logic faulty. After examination of sixty cases of reported cannibalism, he concludes that Lévi-Strauss's boiling-roasting efforts have been undermined by "the natives who have discovered a veritable smorgasbord of ways of preparing people" (1969: 61). Again, agreement is scarce, even among those who share a common theoretical perspective. Medieval scholars encountered similar problems, since an exact count of the number of angels able to dance on the head of a pin is never a simple task.

Finally, occupying the middle theoretical ground are the ever-present classifiers whose main function is the imposition of intellectual order by propounding categories to encompass all possible expressions of a phenomenon. In the case of cannibalism this has generated a typology according to the status of the one consumed. The most generally used taxonomy includes (1) endocannibalism, which refers to eating a member of one's own group; (2) exocannibalism, indicating the consumption of outsiders; and (3) autocannibalism, signifying ingesting parts of one's own body, if that can be imagined. In this final instance, when an individual is forced to eat part of his own flesh, the cannibal and the victim become one and the same.

The classificatory situation is compounded by cross-cutting typologies according to the motive for the act. This results in the recognition of (1) gastronomic cannibalism, where human flesh is eaten for its taste and food value; (2) ritual or magical cannibalism, identifying an attempt to absorb the spiritual essence of the deceased; and (3) survival cannibalism, indicating a resort to this normally prohibited behavior in crisis conditions. Combining the two systems provides the possibility for the memorable phrase "gastronomic endocannibalism" (Dole 1962: 567), which transforms the act of eating human beings into something almost unpronounceable by the human mouth.

From the seemingly disparate interests and needs of the ecologists, structuralists and classifiers, a number of common characteristics nevertheless emerge. Although there are undoubtedly further coincidences, only three need be of concern here. First there is the basic notion that customary cannibalism not only still exists but once was much more pervasive. Second, the subject matter is mystified by resorting to a specialized vocabulary. In the process, the layman is excluded from participation in a discourse now reserved for "scientists" and must be content to be instructed. Third, the objects of all the intellectual energy (except for survival cannibalism, which is left to popularizing participants) are the primitives. Each of these matters will be of some concern later, but the latter problem, of cannibals and primitives, invites more immediate attention.

Much to our satisfaction, the discussion of cannibalism as a custom is normally restricted to faraway lands just prior to or during their "pacification" by the various agents of western civilization. Explorer, conquistador, missionary, trader and colonizer all play their roles in the civilizing mission. Correspondingly, if the time is lengthened sufficiently back to the pre-Christian era, we permit ourselves a glimpse of this sort of savagery among our own forebears. Cannibalism becomes a feature of the faraway or foregone, which is much the same thing. In the way that the dimensions of time and space are interpreted, "they," in the form of distant cannibals, are reflections of us as we once were.

The credibility of these published accounts diminishes as they begin to impinge upon us culturally and temporally. Rather than permitting cherished ideas to be challenged, reinterpretation or denial of the material is called for. Consequently, the Roman accusation that the emerging Christian sect used blood in mysterious secret rites is dismissed by historians as having been a politically inspired slander. The possibility that early Christians may have been cannibals is never seriously considered. Instead, the idea is assumed to be false. In a similar vein the charges, this time by Christians, that Jews resorted to this practice are now a source of embarrassment to liberal thinkers. These accusations were so numerous, widespread and persistent that in this century a non-Jewish German scholar (Strack 1909) who wrote on this phenomenon actually entitled one chapter of his book "Is the Use of Christian Blood Required or Allowed for Any Rite Whatever of the Jewish Religion?" This is followed by a sober assessment of Jewish dietary strictures, including the prohibition on the use of animal blood, which the author contends would also hold for the vital fluid of Christians. Today, this question is banished from our consciousness, and beliefs such as these are interpreted as regrettable temporary lapses into prejudice. Strack prefaces his enumeration and commentary on dozens of reported accusations with the hopeful remark: "The long list of 'ritual murders' which terrifies the ignorant will shrink very much in size in the judgement of anyone who seriously weighs all the facts presented here" (178).

In contrast to this critical position, the idea that Africans, Polynesians, New Guineans, American Indians are or were man-eaters until contact with the benefits of European influence is assumed to be in the realm of demonstrated fact. To recapitulate: beliefs of this sort about representatives of our cultural tradition

Fifteenth-century German print depicting the ritual murder of Simon of Trent by Jews for his blood.

are dismissed out of hand as prejudice and racism, while similar notions about others already defined as categorically different from us are treated as facts worthy of further scholarly consideration. Concretely, the widespread African belief that Europeans are cannibals or use human blood for evil intent is interpreted as an indication of African ignorance. As a correlate, the "fact" of

THE MAN-EATING MYTH

African cannibalism is thought to be the result of African igno-rance of civilized standards.

This interpretation resorts to both a single and a double standard. The single constant is African ignorance. The double standard involves the *a priori* dismissal of the existing reports on cannibalism for Europeans and the acceptance of every report for non-European people. There is little science or scholarship in-volved; but a substantial amount of scientism and ethnocentrism is required to arrive at this position. How else can one interpret the fact that despite the long-standing and pervasive assumption of European cannibalism by others and the existence of written reports such as those referred to, the Human Relations Area Files, which are supposed to be a composite of all known culture traits, do not list any European group under the heading "Canni-balism"? On the other hand, a host of non-western groups are listed in this fashion. This compendium is supposed to serve as a repository of knowledge about cultures, so ideally it should men-tion the reports on the Scots, Picts, Irish, Jews and Christians. As a further indication of the nature of the problem, certain non-western groups are listed merely because some travelers have written that the people in question are *not* cannibals; however, it is necessary to refer to the original source to determine this. The standards employed in this instance of scholarship are again of interest and questionable.

This conclusion is based on the fact that, excluding survival conditions, I have been unable to uncover adequate documenta-tion of cannibalism as a custom in any form for any society. Rumors, suspicions, fears and accusations abound, but no satis-factory first-hand accounts. Learned essays by professionals are unending, but the sustaining ethnography is lacking. The argu-ment that a critical re-examination is both a necessary and a profitable exercise is based on the premise that cannibalism by definition is an observable phenomenon. Following this, the evi-dence for its existence should be derived from observation by reliable sources. Again it is worth asking, why is it that an act which is both so fascinating and repugnant to us should merely be assumed to exist rather than documented? This study examines some of the facets of this peculiar situation and suggests that for layman and scholar alike the idea of cannibalism exists prior to and thus independent of the evidence. I have marshaled the available material to support this premise, rather than manipulating the data to generate the kind of foregone conclusion which characterizes the present thinking on this topic.

In the following pages a brief examination is offered of some first-hand tales of cannibalism which would initially seem to undermine the position taken here. However, these accounts also illustrate how seemingly concrete evidence turns out to be quite unsatisfactory and unable to stand up to an analysis which makes no prior judgments. Less credible examples of cannibal tales are available and could be more deftly dealt with. Admittedly some of these creep into later chapters for the sake of comic relief, but it would not do to start with them.

The initial example is provided by Hans Staden, an extraordinary fellow who visited the South American coast in the mid-sixteenth century as a common seaman on a Portuguese trading ship. Through a series of misfortunes, including shipwreck, he was soon captured by the Tupinamba Indians. As a result of his ill luck, the Tupinamba have come down to us today as man-eaters *par excellence*. Needless to say, the hero was not eaten himself, and after a period of captivity returned to his native Germany, where he published his tale of woe, called: *Hans Staden: The True History and Description of a Country of Savages, A Naked and Terrible People, Eaters of Men's Flesh, who Dwell in the New World called America. Being wholly Unknown in Hesse Both Before and After Christ's Birth Until Two Years Ago, when Hans Staden of Hamberg in Hesse Took Personal Knowledge of Them and Now Presents His Story in Print.* The narrative, with its explicit details, is interspersed with woodcuts displaying the cannibalistic bent of the Indians, who were wont to eat their captives. Staden is easily identified in these scenes as the one in the fig leaf with hands clasped in prayer. This material is often referred to by other writers in more abstract discourses on cannibalism, so it justly deserves closer scrutiny.

According to Staden in a chapter devoted to this topic, a captive is maintained as both prisoner and guest for a period. In addition to food and shelter, he is also provided with the comforts of a female companion. If the woman becomes pregnant as the result, the child is raised as one of them, but during adulthood, "when the mood seizes them, they kill and eat it" (1928: 155). Our hero was among them for less than twelve months, and therefore could not have observed this entire process, so there is no way of knowing the origin of this informational aside. Meanwhile, preparations are made for the victim's ultimate demise and consumption. Food and drink are prepared, guests invited, and the unfortunate fellow led through a number of "warm-up" sessions as "the women bring forth the prisoner once or twice to the place where he is to die and dance around him" (156). On the day of the big event, he is brought, bound, to the appointed spot, where in front of the assembly he is further taunted by the painted females, who boast that they will eat him. The victim suffers further mental anguish at their hands. They build a fire near him, and display the club that will shortly be used to dispatch him to his ancestors. Finally, he is executed by a male warrior and the "women seize the body at once." After it is butchered, four of their number, with the respective limbs in their possession, run around the village "making a joyful cry" (161). The body is then cooked and devoured with apparent relish, according to Staden, who says: "I was present and have seen all this with my own eyes" (162).

This statement is immediately followed by a small paragraph which curiously informs the reader that "the savages have not the art of counting beyond five" (162). Consequently, they often have to resort to their fingers and toes. In those instances when higher mathematics are involved extra hands and feet are called in to assist in the enumeration. What the author is attempting to

convey in his simple way with this addendum is that the Tupi-namba lack culture in the sense of basic intellectual abilities. The inability to count is to him supportive documentation for the idea that these savages would resort to cannibalism. To Staden and many others, eating human flesh implies an animal nature which would be accompanied by the absence of other traits of "real" human beings who have a monopoly on culture. More will be said about this later; my immediate concern is with Staden's "eye-witness" account. If the material is considered in a broader context, certain problems arise.

It is doubtful whether Staden, as a common seaman of the sixteenth century, actually wrote the book himself, and ghost-writers were not unknown even in this earliest era of publishing. The preface to the original by Dr. John Dryander, a professor of medicine at the university in Marburg, suggests a collaboration of some sort between the two. The woodcuts in the book were prepared by another specialist. At best, the final product was produced under Staden's supervision, and some nine years after his return to Europe. Therefore we are not dealing with the work of a single individual trained in the craft of ethnography, but rather with a committee, only one of whom was on the scene.

There are also the matters of language and ability to recollect to be considered. In one instance, the narrator ruefully mentions being unable to communicate his plight to a Frenchman who visited his captors' settlement. Apparently he had no facility in the language of his fellow European. However, Staden is able to provide the details of numerous conversations among the Indians themselves, even though he was with them for a relatively limited period. He is particularly adept at recounting verbatim the Indian dialogue on the very first day of his captivity, as they discussed among themselves how, when and where they would eat Staden. Obviously, he could not have understood the language at the time, and was reconstructing the scene as he imagined it nine

Scenes from Hans Staden representing the cannibal nature of the Tupinamba and the author's tribulations among them.

years before. The later dialogues in the text must have also been a reconstruction, since there is no indication he kept notes, even if he could write. In one scene, which stands as a testimony to Staden's memory and piety, he repeats the psalm "Out of the depths have I cried unto thee." The Indians respond: "See how he cries; now he is sorrowful indeed" (67). One would have to assume that the Indians also had a flair for languages in order to understand and respond to Staden's German so quickly. In summary, there was great opportunity for a certain degree of embellishment by the author, as well as by his colleagues in the eventual publishing venture.

The final objection is a more subtle one, and refers to Staden's representation of the sexes. As the previous quotes indicate, the Tupinamba women are the worst culprits in Staden's version. They debase the noble captive who meets his fate at the hands of another male in an honorable fashion. Further, although Staden makes it clear that women cook and eat human flesh, he is not as explicit about the involvement of males. The woodcuts, illustrating the actual consumption of the human meal in a most graphic manner, show primarily women and children engaged in the act. The females are represented in both prose and illustrations as the most savage of the savages. This parallels the data to be discussed later from New Guinea, where the women are also portrayed as the main cannibalistic culprits. It is important to remember that very often stereotyped cultural sexual antagonism is expressed in references to the vile nature of the opposite gender. As we are all too well aware from our knowledge of both simple and complex societies, prejudices depicting the unsavory nature of a minority have little if any bearing on empirical reality. Instead, such caricatures function as ideological props in a system of repression in the service of the majority. In the case of the Tupinamba, as well as in other simple social systems, which lack other significant internal divisions, this normally involves male dominance with attending notions of female inferiority which the women earn by their assumed inherent uncultured behavior. As a relevant aside, it is worth mentioning that these very same Tupinamba were a primary source of information on the legendary Amazon society of Brazil. Native informants were apparently quite explicit about the existence and customs of this mythical violent all-female society, which received males as visitors only for the sake of reproduction. It was said that male offspring were given to their assumed fathers when they returned the following year, or even worse, they were immediately killed (Markham 1964: 117–23). The Tupinamba imagination lacked little in the way of inventing a barbaric, uncultured view of female nature.

It would be misleading to suggest that Staden alone is responsible for our knowledge of Tupinamba cannibalism, or the only source of information on their practice. He was not even the first, for the idea that the Brazilian Indians were man-eaters preceded Staden by some time. Indeed the earliest known, if not the first, representation of American Indians, dating from 1505 in the form of a European engraving, depicts one of the characters contentedly gnawing away on a human arm while other parts of the body are roasting over a fire (Eames 1922). The description of a subsequently added text of unknown origin accompanying the woodcut contains further ethnographic gems worth recalling in full. It states:

This figure represents to us the people and island which have been discovered by the Christian King of Portugal or by his subjects. The people are thus naked, handsome, brown, well shaped in body, their heads, necks, arms, private parts, feet of men and women are a little covered with feathers. The men also have many precious stones in their faces and breasts. No one also has anything, but all things are in common. And the men have as wives those who please them, be they mothers, sisters, or friends, therein make they no distinction. They also fight with each other. They also eat each other even those who are slain, and hang the flesh of them in the smoke. They become a hundred and fifty years old. And have no government [756].

ANTHROPOLOGY AND ANTHROPOPHAGY   27

The entire paragraph is a mine of amazing misinformation, but there are two points worthy of comment. First, the written detail is self-contradictory, since it states that the Indians both go about naked and wear gems and feathers. It also fails to correspond to the picture, which shows everyone sporting some sort of garment below the waist. Second, the commentary makes the familiar connection between incest and cannibalism. The significance of this equation will become more evident later, so it is sufficient to suggest now that the images of nakedness, indiscriminate sexual liaisons and cannibalism are meant to convey the idea that the Indians are more akin to animals than culture-bearing human beings. The main point is that Staden and other seafarers of the time were most likely already convinced of Tupinamba savagery and cannibalism before they set foot on the continent, since the idea already had currency.

What about those who came after Staden, whose written works also confirm the Tupinamba practice? The essence of the scientific method is the ability of others to verify the data independently, so that the existence of further accounts from the same era should make for a conclusive case of customary cannibalism. It would be unreasonable to imply out of hand that they all misrepresented their observations; but they might have resorted to a common shortcoming of authors both past and present called plagiarism. A return to Staden's account is necessary to reconstruct the events and argument.

In his chapter on killing and eating the victim, Staden supplies some further Indian dialogue which he translates for his readers. He states that the Indian who is about to slay the prisoner says to him: "I am he that will kill you, since you and yours have slain and eaten many of my friends." The prisoner replies: "When I am dead I shall still have many to avenge my death" (161). Dismissing the linguistic barrier momentarily, and assuming Staden to be an adept translator of this language, the presentation of the actual words of the characters lends an aura of authenticity to the events. However, if similar phrases begin to make

The earliest known portrayal of the inhabitants of the New World: a sixteenth-century woodcut depicting cannibalism and "free love" among the South American Indians.

their appearance in the accounts of others who put themselves forward as eyewitnesses to similar deeds, then the credibility of the confirmation process diminishes. For example, Las Casas, in his *History of the Indies,* also written in the sixteenth century, reproduces a letter from some unnamed Portuguese priests among the Tupinamba who describe the cannibalistic rite and point out that the victim says to his executioner "that in his day he too killed his enemies, and that his relatives remain to avenge his death" (1971: 68). In an account by André Thevet, a French visitor to the Tupinamba whose tract was soon translated into English, we learn that he also witnessed the same scene, and this time the victim says: "I have killed and eaten his parents and friends, to whom I am prisoner." He adds: "Neither will the Margaiates suffer my death unrevenged" (1568: 707). Then there are the literary reminiscences of the same era of another Frenchman in Brazil who also reports on Tupinamba cannibalism. Again the reporter is able to recall the words of the slayer, who this time says: "N'es-tu pas de la nation nommée Margaias, qui nous est ennemie? n'as-tu pas toy-mesme tué & mangé de nos parens & amis?" (Léry 1780: 45). ("Are you not of the nation called Margaias, who are our enemies? Have you not killed and eaten our parents and friends?") Finally, to round out the list, we encounter a sixteenth-century English observer of the very same deed, who this time reports the Tupinamba saying to a recently captured Portuguese victim: "I am he that hath killed many of thy Nation and will kill thee" (Knivet 1906: 222).

Because of the difficulty of establishing the exact publication dates of the works cited above, it is not always possible to determine who is paraphrasing whom. However, it is abundantly clear that the later authors are taking some liberties with Staden's account of the scene without giving him due credit for having propounded this dramatic little scene and dialogue in the first instance. Plagiarism of this sort, which has been documented for other times and places (cf. Jenkins 1968 and Evans-Pritchard 1965), was fairly common in the reports of travelers to foreign lands as a result of the desire not to be outdone by the colorful accounts of other sojourners.

Rejecting the plagiarism hypothesis put forward here would require instead accepting the proposition that a parade of international travelers all passed through a Tupinamba encampment on different days when the Indians were about to slay a war captive while the main characters were repeating similar statements to each other. If this should be insufficient cause for doubt about the veracity of the accounts, it must also be remembered that these English, French and Portuguese passersby would have to have been as fluent in Tupinamba as the German Hans Staden in order to translate the conversation between the two Indians. The notion that a number of authors were copying from each other should not be accepted lightly in considering the question

THE MAN-EATING MYTH

of independent verification of historical evidence if other, more reasonable, explanations are available. However, in this instance, the peculiar content of the published material, taken together with the linguistic problems involved, leads to the conclusion that plagiarism is the simplest and most likely explanation for the consistency of the data.

For the case of the Tupinamba, this means that, rather than dealing with an instance of serial documentation of cannibalism, we are more likely confronting only one source of dubious testimony which has been incorporated almost verbatim into the written reports of others claiming to be eyewitnesses. Thus, rather than the scientific procedure of independent verification, we have instead an instance of its scholarly antithesis being used to construct a case for an assumed well-established instance of customary cannibalism for a traditional South American Indian culture.

Finally, it must be added that these famous cannibals, who were supposed to make others disappear into their cooking pots, have instead themselves vanished. As a result of their contact with and treatment by Europeans who were so quick to label them man-eaters, the Tupinamba failed to survive the sixteenth century. As a result, there is no modern information on the traditional culture of this group. Although there may be some legitimate reservations about who ate whom, there can be none on the question of who exterminated whom.

The next eyewitness accout of cannibalism for the other side of the world is taken from the nineteenth-century experiences of Ta'unga, another extraordinary traveler. A native Polynesian from the island of Rarotonaga, Ta'unga was converted to Christianity and subsequently became an evangelist for the London Mission Society, which had a main outpost on his island. Recently, a collection of his reports to his supervisors on his experiences on outlying islands, originally written in his native language, has become available. His accounts, based on his experiences as an advance man for European missionaries in the

Pacific, are truly blood-curdling. They suggest a brand of cannibalism in the extreme, as compared to the relatively mild situation prevailing among the Tupinamba.

If one is willing to believe the author, cannibalism was an everyday affair on the islands of New Caledonia. Rather than a special ritual event, as in the previous instance, the consumption of human flesh was a matter of course as the result of the desire for meat. For this very reason, Ta'unga writes, "the inhabitants never stop fighting, day and night, month in and month out" (Crocombe 1968: 86). Not far beyond the skirmish lines, the women lie in wait to snatch up the bodies of the slain enemies. If none become available, they just as eagerly drag away and cut up for meat the corpses of their own warriors. In the words of Ta'unga, which might have just as easily been written by Staden, the women did this "shouting with glee because their wants have been satisfied" (87). It is difficult to imagine how long a human population could sustain itself on a single island beset with constant warfare and cannibalism, but apparently there was no problem, since this was only the tip of the iceberg.

In ominous tones, our missionary reporter announces to his superiors on the home island and in London that human beings "are like fish to them," "so that not only victims taken in war are eaten" (90). Indeed, the list is endless, for everyone is a potential meal for someone else. More ghastly is the information that not only enemies see each other on the menu. A mere argument between two acquaintances will result in one being killed and then "brought in for cooking." In an atmosphere which would transform Cain into a paragon of virtue, even brothers who have a falling-out will not be loath to make a meal of each other. However, this is still not the bottom rung, for we learn that parents will do the same to their child, except that, for some inexplicable reason, only the head is eaten.

Ta'unga dutifully mentions that he tried to persuade the locals to abandon these horrid customs, but they took no notice of him. It is difficult to refute this evidence, but on the other hand it would be even more difficult to accept it at face value as the truth. Although the account might have conformed to certain nineteenth-century ideas about the state of humanity without the benefits of a Christian education, it does not accord with a century of experience accumulated by anthropologists on the human condition. The comment by a student of the first-hand reports of Jewish cannibal rites is instructive here. Unable to refute centuries-old descriptions, he concluded that it was impossible to do more than be astounded by the manner in which the products of an excited imagination were once accepted as facts (Strack 1909: 33).

It should also be remembered that not too long ago there were stories of Amazons, people who lived in trees, others with their heads between their shoulders and their feet on backwards. The assumed species *Homo monstrosus* did not become extinct as a scientific notion until the last century (Malefijt 1968), and there are still certain folk survivals in the form of the Himalayan Snowman and related types. The existence of normal physical types whose only failing was cannibalism was not too incredible. To some, the deductive arguments brought to bear against these cannibal accusations will be insufficient counters to the personal narratives. To those, another, more concrete, question might well be posed. If the natives of New Caledonia ate everyone, from distant enemy to close kin, then how did Ta'unga escape this fate? Any missionary would be able to answer this query, but would resorting to divine intervention be sufficient for the more objective analyst?

There is a further test of the data which, as in the case of the Tupinamba, involves an evaluation of its internal consistency. This requires consideration of further detail in Ta'unga's story.

Before bringing to a close the section "On the Eating of Men," Ta'unga plays on the reader's emotions with one final nerve-wracking scene, accompanied by a drawing of the event. The story was put down some time after the author's visit to the island, since it is prefaced by the statement "There is something

Print from *The Works of Ta'unga*, showing the choice of a cannibal victim in the South Pacific.

which I forgot to write about previously" (Crocombe 1968: 93). The original version of this tale and the drawing first appeared in a missionary mazagine in 1848, with the caption "Missionary representation of the son of Pasan asking his father for the fat men to eat" (94). The representative of European civilization appears in the background more fully clothed than his local companions. Curiously enough his hands are clasped in prayer. The pathetic tableau involves a transcript-like account of a conversation between a local chief and his favorite son. Having decided on the individual, the father asks the boy if he wants the victim dispatched at once. The child replies: "Cut him up alive." This is followed by a further transcript and a vivid account of the piecemeal destruction of the poor victim. Ta'unga goes on to inform his pastor and European readers: "I was overcome with grief and tried to stop them, but they would not listen because I did not know their language, so I was unable to tell them of the right way of life" (93). The obvious question is again prompted. With this linguistic incapacity, how was it possible for the reporter to repeat even the gist of a conversation in an unknown dialect? Ta'unga may have been a staunch representative of the faith, but he was hardly one of the original twelve apostles possessing the gift of tongues.

The two accounts of cannibalism reviewed here leave something to be desired, both in terms of the particulars of the presumed events and the general atmosphere. Each makes some contribution to our knowledge of other cultures as they existed in the past, but as complete works they are too biased and unsophisticated to be accepted as credible portraits of other peoples. Too many of their remarks on other aspects of these societies are so naive, in light of our present understanding of cultural phenomena, as to be of little use. In addition, for its own reasons each book aims to depict the inhabitants in accordance with the then-prevailing notions of savagery. These images are not too far removed from present standards, and provide a context in which the account of cannibalism and views of a contemporary anthropologist can best be appreciated.

Claims of having observed cannibalism first-hand are rampant in the travelogues of explorers, missionaries, traders and others of the same ilk. Naturally enough, these testimonies vary in detail. At one pole are the oblique observations by early wanderers passing through villages of peoples they had heard were hardened man-eaters that, true enough, human flesh was seen over the cooking fire (cf. Weeks 1913). At the other extreme are the graphic memoirs of Staden and Ta'unga, which must be treated with more care. The former type, which are interspersed throughout this study, earn little if any credibility.

Leaving this brand of literature behind, and examining instead the production of professional anthropologists, the problems change but the situation still remains perplexing. From all corners of the globe the reports come in that a specific group of people an anthropologist has lived among were cannibals long ago, before contact, until pacification, just recently or only yesterday. The reader is engulfed by a stream of past tenses denoting varying removes in time, indicating a demise of the custom sometime before the researcher took up residence on the scene. As indicated earlier, there are scores of articles devoted to the subject of anthropophagy. The strange part is that a long-standing interest in this topic has turned up only one publication by an anthropologist who claims to have actually witnessed the event. All the others, even those with the word cannibalism in the title, qualify, hedge, or are couched in the past tense until it eventually becomes clear that the anthropologist did not actually see the event being described. A careful reading of the material suggests that, rather than trying to delude the reader, the author is so convinced of the validity of the assumption that the distortion is not consciously perceived. I propose this after considerable research, which has involved following up on the claims of colleagues that they have read first-hand accounts composed by other anthropologists. These turn out to be in the same non-event category described above. Therefore, the chance to consider even a brief account from the present is a rare opportunity.

This article, which, according to a footnote, was first presented as a lecture and illustrated by motion pictures and slides, starts out commonly enough with the statement: "The eating of human flesh by human beings has been extremely widespread" (Dole 1962: 567). The immediately following section proposes the "endocannibalism, exocannibalism, autocannibalism" schema alluded to earlier. The disappearance of the custom among other people is explained in terms of the "tireless efforts" of European agents. In a breakdown of normal standards of neutrality which is often characteristic of anthropological discussions of this phenomenon, ritual endocannibalism is defined as restricted to "uncivilized peoples" (567). However, the main purpose of the publication is the description and analysis of a particular type of "bone ash" cannibalism supposedly still extant in the present era among

THE MAN-EATING MYTH

the Amahuaca Indians of the Peruvian-Brazilian border. As a rare example of observed "ritual endocannibalism," even in such an esoteric form, the material deserves detailed presentation.

During one night, a young infant died, and amidst mourning by the closest kin and the respectful demeanor of other villagers, the child was buried in a shallow grave. The body was encased in a coffin made from cooking pots held together with twine. These also contained some items associated with the child, such as rags, a hammock, and corncob amusements. The mother visited the grave daily with outward expressions of her grief and on the seventh day, as is the custom, the body was disinterred for the purposes of cremation. Firewood, made from the grinding trough of the mother, which was expressly split for this purpose, and other kindling was placed around the unopened pots containing the deceased and set ablaze. After some time the pots were opened and extra wood added to finish the process. After cooling had taken place, the mother removed the tiny bits of bones which remained. The pots and ashes were then returned to the grave and covered over again. At this point, it will be best to provide the author's own text, which follows the actions of Yamba Wachi, the mother of the child.

Yamba Wachi continued to wail intermittently a few more days, holding the bowl of bones on her lap. During this time her adult son cut a new trough. When finished, she ground corn and made gruel. Into this she mixed the bone powder and drank the mixture (569).

Notice the problem. In one sentence the bone bits are concrete, and in the very next one they are powder. There is no indication by Dole how, where or why the bones were turned into this powdery substance. This is a glaring omission in an otherwise extremely meticulous rendering of a funerary ceremony which is supposed to culminate in cannibalism. If the author did indeed see the bones ground into a powder, why is this not mentioned in the text? If she did not see this action take place, then how is it possible to say that the powder was actually the ground bones of the child? There is no doubt we are dealing with a complicated process reminiscent of the shell game, except in this instance a pot and bones are the constantly shifting items. The bones could easily get lost even from the eye of the trained observer, who sees them in one instant but in the next does not. The native hand turns out to be quicker than the anthropologist's eye.

The reader who thinks this sort of careful combing of the material is uncalled-for should remember that this is the one and only description by an anthropologist who explicitly claims to have actually witnessed cannibalism. If the custom of eating the dead was well documented and confirmed independently by others, then such an approach as the one guiding this study would be unnecessarily tedious. However, this sort of intellectual security is lacking. Instead of a demonstrated fact, we constantly encounter assumption and rumor and the fear these might be true. Therefore, a rigorous interpretation demands that the one and only account offered as concrete evidence for ritual cannibalism contain no gaps, especially at the crucial point of consumption. At this very juncture, the description breaks down so that the reader is forced to close the gap and assume he has read a detailed account of cannibalism, when in fact this is not the case. Instead the reader is asked to make the same basic initial assumption as the author that cannibalism is pervasive and this is just another instance. Rather than this material being used to support the idea that cannibalism exists, the opposite is the case. The prior belief in the existence of the custom is the necessary first step for accepting this account. It is not possible to state with any degree of certainty that the Amahuaca do not practice "bone ash ritual endocannibalism," nor can it be said with any assurance that they do. As usual, we are left with doubts and a mystery.

Another striking omission in Dole's account is the failure to consider any of the symbolic elements of this extended ceremony. Such an analysis is best undertaken on the basis of a personal experience with the culture or through intellectual immersion in an extensive body of published literature. In light of limited ethnographic material in Dole's essay, only a simple suggestion can be offered. Such an analysis would immediately seize upon the significance of the grinding trough. Excluding the deceased, the central figure in the ceremony is the mother, and the central object is the trough, likely to be strongly associated with motherhood. The trough is destroyed in the same fire which consumes the child, simultaneously indicating the demise of her major roles as child-rearer and provider. In effect, the mother's social personality is laid to rest along with the mixture of the ashes of her child and domestic implements. Her mourning soon comes to an end and she re-emerges when another of her sons prepares a new trough. This is used to create a meal from corn and, in Dole's account, the bones of her dead son. As Dole concludes: "The mother continued to mourn until she had consumed the last vestiges of the infant, whereupon her attitude changed radically, as had her husband's earlier. She became voluble and happy, with no suggestion of her bereavement" (569). The most important point is whether she actually consumed the bone powder or whether ground corn was a symbolic substitute. This is not as improbable as it might first seem, since the substitution of a significant item of food for a spirit is a widespread cultural trait. When such an incident of transubstantiation occurs, it is best to consider a symbolic analysis as the proper mode of interpretation. This is suggested in spite of the native's likely insistence that the actual act of eating human flesh has taken place.

Additional ethnographic data on the Amahuaca would be necessary to build a stronger case for a symbolic interpretation. The production of corn as an important female activity is a safe assumption, and greater detail on this matter would likely provide further support for considering the fertility element ingrained in the funerary events. The customs attending on the death of an adult would also be helpful, for it is unlikely that the same sequence of acts would be performed. However, in the end this would still be irrelevant, since the major points of contention are unaffected. These involve the crucial gap in Dole's description of the observable events and the complete failure to consider the symbolic element of the ritual.

This chapter, with its introduction to the nature of the discipline and the problem, sets the stage for more important topics to be considered in succeeding sections. The primary purpose thus far has been to show that the pervasive data about the cannibalistic nature of others bears little if any relationship to the method of objective scientific inquiry. Careful scrutiny of some of the best instances of what is put forward as "observed" cannibalism reveals the nature of the evidence. These examples were primarily accounts by single individuals of what were presented as isolated events among obscure peoples on the fringes of time and space. What follows in the next chapters is the analysis of material from numerous scholars and various disciplines. These instances involve reported wide-scale cannibalism among peoples who figure heavily in our view of the social universe, with particular reference to the boundary between civilized and savage.

THE
CLASSIC
MAN—EATERS

The standard procedure in an academic exercise of this type usually involves a judicious harvest of bits and pieces of information from numerous scattered human groups (sometimes referred to as "tribe trotting") in order to prove or disprove a point of the author's choosing. As erudite as this may appear, the apt-example method has little else to recommend it. The reader is overwhelmed and forced into a passive role by a barrage of minutiae on customs from societies with unpronounceable names. The composite picture which is carefully drawn for the reader may be pleasing or displeasing, depending upon predispositions. However, the conclusions cannot be evaluated properly unless the reader is prepared to undertake a similar intellectual odyssey. Faith and trust may be admirable qualities in other contexts, but they are not appropriate in a situation such as this. A related methodological problem is the inability of either the researcher or reader to fully comprehend the significance of a single custom or informant's statement which is artificially divorced from its cultural milieu. Social action or ideas can only be appreciated in the context of the cultural system of which they form a part. In isolation the interpretation of such facts is sometimes meaningless and at other times misleading.

In an effort to overcome some of these defects, this and the following chapter will focus on a limited number of cases which normally figure prominently in any discussion of cannibalism. The anthropophagic act, as it has been told and retold by a series of reporters from varying distances and perspectives, will be considered in a broad cultural context. In addition, this orientation will consider the context of the reporting by attempting to understand as best as possible the temper of the times in the western world. More often it is awareness of the intellectual atmosphere on the receiving end which is most helpful in evaluating and interpreting the evidence. The anthropologist and the anthropophagist are worthy of similar consideration.

Until the end of the fifteenth century the literal term *anthropophagist* described those savages on the fringes of western civilization who partook of human flesh. However, the fifteenth century came to a close as an age with seemingly unending opportunities for terminological and geographical expansion with the discovery of the New World and its—on first reports—often astounding inhabitants. Thus it is only fitting that the first case study should be provided by the Caribs, from whom the more recent word, *cannibal,* is derived via Spanish. Through Spanish mispronunciation, Caribs became Canibs and eventually cannibals. The Caribs owe the distinction of having their name serve as the modern English synonym for man-eater to none other than Christopher Columbus. The facts that only his ship, the *Santa Maria,* sank on the first outward journey, that his second ran aground on his return trip to the New World, and that he died still believing he had discovered a new route to Cathay do not mean we should pay little heed to his opinions, but these facts do immediately demystify the Great Navigator. Although Columbus heard the rumors from others he failed to see any direct evidence, so he actually did not believe the Caribs were cannibals; however he was not above spreading the idea of New World man-eating creatures throughout Europe on his return from the fantastic journey. An appreciation of this situation requires some ethnographic and historic details for one of the most eventful eras of world history.

With the discovery of a New World to the west and the recent invention of the printing press, the sixteenth-century dawned with a veritable explosion of potential knowledge. The possibilities for the dissemination of errors and thus the spread of a new kind of ignorance also expanded apace. The information on the topic of man-eating illustrates clearly enough that both processes took place with equal facility. On the other side of the

"Ocean Sea" a similar penchant for misinformation prevailed among the natives. More often than not these various prejudices criss-crossed the Atlantic to become part of common knowledge.

The islands with which Columbus first came into contact were inhabited by the Arawaks and Caribs, two distinct culture groups. The Northern Islands, which include Cuba, Puerto Rico, Santo Domingo and the Bahamas, with minor exceptions were inhabited by the Arawak, who spoke similar dialects of a mother tongue and shared other social and cultural patterns. Their world-view apparently included a hatred and fear of the Caribs, their more aggressive and different neighbors on the smaller islands to the south, such as St. Vincent, St. Croix and Martinique. The word for man-eater is now cannibal and not "arawakibal, because Columbus first encountered the latter, who were eager to fill him in on the gossip about their enemies to the south. However, there was more than local slander which led the Europeans who were to follow to accept this appellation for the southern natives. According to Columbus in a partial transcript of his journal (the complete original has been lost), the Arawak were a gentle and peaceful people who greeted their European visitors with hospitality. Columbus repaid the compliment by reporting to Ferdinand and Isabel that these Arawaks "are fitted to be ruled and to be set to work, to cultivate the land and do all else that may be necessary . . ." (1968: 101–2). His failure to return with the spices and gold he had promised may have had something to do with Columbus's veiled hints about the potential profits to be had from slavery. He also informed their majesties that he "understood" from a conference with these Arawaks many other interesting beliefs. They told him that to the south "there were men with one eye, and others with dogs' noses, who ate men, and that when they took a man, they cut off his head and drank his blood and castrated him" (52). They were also the consorts of Amazons, for he was further informed that these very same cannibals were the ones "who have intercourse with the women of 'Martino' . . . in which there is not a man" (200).

THE CLASSIC MAN-EATERS   45

It is not obvious today how Columbus came to understand this information, since his only interpreter was an Arabic-speaking Jew who had been expelled from Spain in 1492 on the *Santa Maria*. Possibly the Arawak were kinder in their description of the Caribs and some of the more fanciful comments might be laid to translation problems. Further, Columbus scoffed at these stories, commenting that the natives also first thought he and his men were cannibals (68–69). However, his journal, which was a day-by-day account of his expedition, was never published intact. Apparently afraid that the Portuguese would get their hands on this informative document, Ferdinand and Isabel refused to permit its publication. However, as one biographer puts it, "with Marco Polo humming in his head and the vague syllables of the savages buzzing in his ears, putting two and two together and persuading himself that the two ends of the earth have met" (Brooks 1924: vii–viii), he published a brief account of his journey to the land of the "Great Khan." In this letter, which was immediately translated and printed throughout Europe, Columbus presented a summary of some of the more colorful aspects of his journey, including the unqualified statement that some of the islands were inhabited by man-eaters called Caribs (Columbus 1968: 200). Apparently, the temptation was too much for him and the Carib reputation was set for time immemorable.

In a manner befitting his new rank, "Admiral of the Ocean Sea and Viceroy of the Indies," Columbus returned to the New World in the following year with seventeen ships and fifteen hundred men. In addition to bringing greater numbers of soldiers and provisions, the armada intended to colonize as well as explore. The "pacification" of the previously unsighted Caribs was a high priority, so that the fleet made its first landfall on the unknown southern islands. In what must have come as a surprise to the admiral, the Caribs of Guadaloupe fled from their villages at the sight of the Spaniards. Possibly they had also heard of the existence of man-eaters on distant islands. However, a landing party returned from the deserted villages, claiming that they saw human

Canibalium

Illustration from a seventeenth-century edition of *The Journal of Christopher Columbus*, making the visual equation between native resistance and the cannibal label.

bones in the houses. They also brought with them some Arawak women, who had been kidnapped by the Caribs. Upon direct questioning, they confirmed the rumor that their captors were man-eaters. According to Las Casas (1971: 43–44), who is responsible for preserving what we know of the log, Columbus still privately failed to give credence to such horror stories. Although he may have been dubious at this point, his next stop on St. Croix may have underscored the value of a cannibal rationale. In this instance, which turned out to be the more typical response to Spanish landings, rather than retreating the Caribs attacked the interlopers. The task force then moved on to the more hospitable climes of Hispaniola, in order to establish a base of operations for further exploration of the remaining islands and pacification of the Caribs. The quest for spices and gold was still a failure, so that the slave trade assumed even greater potential significance. The first Caribs captured were sent to Spain with a message from Columbus that he was doing so for the sake of their souls. He then added obliquely: "The welfare of the said Cannibals . . . has raised the thought the more that may be sent over the better" (quoted in Sauer 1966: 77). Thus in his public statements he continued to cultivate the cannibal theme as the possibility of a slave trade assumed greater prominence. By his third voyage, Columbus had become so experienced in these matters that he was able to identify man-eaters by their looks. Thus, he wrote of the natives of the coast of Honduras: "I found another people who eat humans, as the hideousness of their appearance shows" (Sauer 1966: 137).

As these tales were told and retold in Spain, they took on a fantastic and even a more vivid flavor. The Vatican representative to the court of Castile took down the stories from returning travelers in an amazing document now referred to as *De Orbe Novo* (D'Anghera 1912). As single dispatches they were copied and circulated throughout Europe, where they were considered the literary event of the sixteenth century. The Pope had them read aloud to his guests over dinner for their enlightenment. The cannibal nature of the Caribs of course figured prominently in these accounts, so that from the safety of Castile, D'Anghera could report that the first time these savages laid eyes on the Spaniards, "their mouths watered like tavern trenchermen" (402). Since sailors will be sailors, he also informed His Holiness of mermaids, giants, people who lived in trees, islands inhabited by Amazon women who were visited annually by cannibals for the purpose of procreation, and—although he was incredulous about this for a while—people who trained hunting fish. The latter, the most fascinating creatures of the New World, were attached to

THE MAN-EATING MYTH

leashes while they swam next to their master's canoe until they were released to capture other fish. However, D'Anghera drew the line on a story which claimed the existence of a race of men with scaly tails requiring them to dig little holes in the ground before they could sit. This vignette was purveyed at court by a young Indian transported from North America. His stories led one sensible figure in attendance to opine that others listened to him as if he were one of the original twelve apostles (Sauer 1971: 71). All of this is amusing and harmless from the perspective of the European world, but a refocus on the islands of the Caribbean presents a different picture. In due time, as Columbus intimated they would be in his first journal, the natives were put to work in Spanish enterprises.

An administrative system was established giving settlers large grants of land along with the Indian inhabitants for mining and agricultural projects. The more tractable Arawak at first submitted to these arrangements, but then often revolted in the face of the inhumanity of the system. These uprisings were met by the Spanish overlords with greater brutality, which included burning the leaders at the stake. A contemporary historian estimates that between 1494 and 1508 more than three million natives died on Santo Domingo alone as the result of Spanish pacification (Sauer 1966: 155). Even greater doses of hostility were meted out to the Caribs, who resisted colonization and in the process earned further enmity as man-eaters. According to Las Casas, who accompanied Columbus on one expedition and spent a lifetime on the islands before turning to religion and a defense of the Indian cause, any resistance to Spanish colonization was laid to the cannibals (1971: 126). Resistance and cannibalism became synonymous and also legitimized the barbaric Spanish reaction.

The official royal policy initially prohibited the enslavement of the inhabitants of the islands, since their spiritual welfare was considered paramount over the economic interests of the colonialists. Despite protests and violations of the rules by the Europeans on the scene, the monarchs adhered to this policy except in

THE CLASSIC MAN-EATERS   49

Artists' representations from the sixteenth century of the mythical
all-female Amazon society of South America, illustrating
both their amorous and aggressive intentions toward males.

the case of "a certain people called Cannibals." The royal proclamation of 1503 continued:

> if said Cannibals continue to resist and do not wish to admit
> and receive my Captains and men who may be on such
> voyages by my orders nor to hear them in order to be taught
> our Sacred Catholic Faith and to be in my service and
> obedience, they may be captured and are taken to these my
> kingdoms and Domains and to other parts and places and be
> sold [Sauer 1966: 162].

THE MAN-EATING MYTH

The expected scramble for the profit to be made in human bondage followed immediately. Islands once thought to be inhabited by Arawak upon closer investigation turned out in reality to be overrun by hostile cannibals. Slowly but surely greater areas were recognized as Carib and their enslavement legalized (Newson 1976: 72). Thus the operational definition of cannibalism in the sixteenth century was resistance to foreign invasion followed by being sold into slavery, which was held to be a higher status than freedom under aboriginal conditions.

THE CLASSIC MAN-EATERS   51

Although eventually brought under Spanish control and shipped to distant islands to work the mines and plantations of their Spanish masters, the Caribs resorted to passive resistance to forestall complete cultural domination. They turned out to be poor slaves with an indomitable will, which sometimes drove them to suicide rather than accept servitude. Further, they refused to accept the religion of their conquerors. Some of the last pure remnants of Carib culture on St. Vincent had still denied Christianity by the beginning of the eighteenth century. More than that, the missionaries were forced to evacuate the island upon learning of a plot to kill them. On Dominica, twenty-five years of labor in the vineyards produced no converts to Christianity (Sheldon 1820: 410–12). In general, the Spanish failed to realize their dreams of wealth on the islands but managed to eradicate the indigenous peoples and cultures of the Caribbean. Having consumed the Caribs in wars of pacification and in the mines and on the plantations, the Europeans were forced to look to other areas for a continuing source of manpower. Sure enough, they knew of another continent inhabited by similar savages who would be eventually transported to the New World for their own benefit. But cannibalism in Africa must await its turn while we evaluate the evidence on the Caribs, the sixteenth-century prototype of the man-eater.

The contemporary authority on these Indians wrote not too long ago in an article for the educated layman that the Arawak told Columbus they were often subjected to raids by man-eaters called Caribs. The anthropologist-author, citing the journal of Columbus, then adds for the gratification of his readers that "Columbus confirmed the report" that the Caribs "ate captives to absorb their fighting ability" (Rouse 1964: 502). In an early article,

Seventeenth-century engraving suggesting cannibalism for the natives of the island of Española who, before the onset of the slave trade, had not been considered man-eaters.

Rouse wrote with a vividness worthy of a sixteenth-century court chronicler that captured enemies were eaten "with many signs of enjoyment" (1948: 560). Technically, Rouse is correct in his general point, since Columbus did proclaim the savage nature of the Carib, but this is misleading, since Rouse is also aware that Columbus had no evidence for such a confirmation. In fact, as indicated, he did not believe they were actually cannibals, but had a good reason for foisting such an idea on the rulers of Europe. Why a modern academic would continue to propagate such a myth is another problem, to be considered in the final chapter, when the anthropologist and anthropophagist again come under joint scrutiny. However, there is little reason to assume that the very aborigines whose name now means man-eaters actually were so. They may have been hostile to their neighbors, aggressively resisted Spanish imperialism, and preferred their culture to the European, but that is as much as can be said. When one crosses the boundary into an area where ideological justification for inhumanity becomes more important than fact, then much more can be and has been put forward. My position may be the minority viewpoint, but it is not original. Las Casas, a major figure of that era whose accounts are based upon experience in the New World, flatly denies that the Caribs were cannibals (1971). Sheldon (1820), who reviewed the literature at the beginning of the nineteenth century, echoed Las Casas' judgment. Their accounts and arguments rarely find their way into popular forums, since they neither justify the European destruction in the Caribbean nor make such fascinating reading.

After a few decades of Spanish rule, the indigenous cultures of the Caribbean were all but destroyed, but a whole continent still existed to the west. The royal proclamation of 1503 included this area and also legitimized the subjugation of any cannibals to be found there. Some of the expeditions sent to the coast never returned, while others brought back rumors of the continually sought-after riches to be found somewhere in the interior. Having gained valuable experience on what they referred to as *Las Islas*,

THE MAN-EATING MYTH

the Spaniards began to take a more direct interest in *Tierra Firma*. By this time, a young adventurer called Hernando Cortés, when offered a land grant on Santo Domingo, replied that he had come to the New World for gold, not to plant crops. To that end in April 1519 he joined an expedition to the coast and by August of 1520 he was the new Lord of Mexico.

What is now grandly referred to in stirring tones as "The Conquest of Mexico" proves to be one of the many chapters of New World history which contained everything but a hero. The victorious force of six hundred Spaniards was led by Cortés, whose own letters (Cortés 1962) and official biography (Gómara 1964) contain a description of actions which could scarcely be called admirable by the standards of any era. The conquistador proved to be insubordinate and disloyal to his European superiors and a scourge to the Indians. By his own admission he lopped off hands, burned at the stake, ambushed, starved and tortured both high- and low-born natives for the greater glory of God and His Most Catholic Majesty at a genocidal rate. His interest in gold also probably had something to do with his behavior.

The vanquished side was led by the Aztec emperor Montezuma, a passive figure whose most dramatic historical moment was his death. This came at the hands either of his own subjects or of Spaniards, depending upon whose account is read. However, it is clear that both sides had sufficient cause to do him in, since Montezuma was as prone to and almost as adept at double-dealing as Cortés. The difference between the two men in this capacity was the margin between success and failure. The Aztecs were also to pay for their emperor's character flaws, since their subjugation was the eventual result of Montezuma's attempt to delude himself and his subjects about the nature of these visitors. Instead of trying to buy off the Spaniards or imagining them to be the foretold returning gods, he could just as easily have defined them as the cutthroat adventurers they clearly were. No deities, including those familiar to the Aztecs, took such an interest in gold as these pale newcomers. Their human qualities were apparent enough from the first moment of contact with an Aztec provincial official, from whom Cortés demanded in all candor "some gold" to show his good intentions. The Aztec official denied the request, and Cortés left with the prophetic words that Montezuma would soon bid this official acquiesce to the demands of the Spaniards and "give up the gold and what more he had" (Cortés 1962: 39).

Leaving aside the leading personalities and considering instead broader issues, it is tempting to suggest that the phrase "culture shock" be applied to this encounter. The Spaniards, the military representatives of the most powerful nation in Europe, and fresh from the final defeat of the Moors, had invaded the most powerful and vigorous state in North America. The explosive events which followed are also probably the best documented and discussed of the contact era. Numerous accounts are readily available which detail the impressions of Indian and European. The reaction on both sides was one of astonishment as each group struggled to define and comprehend the other's existence in some meaningful way.

The Aztecs were clearly dismayed by the Spanish military hardware and aggressiveness. Their gleaming armor, enormous war dogs, and men on horses which were initially thought to be a single creature amazed the Indians. The possession and use of firearms was beyond their understanding. However, it was the foreigners' previously mentioned interest in precious metal which made the most vivid impression on the natives. An anonymous Indian informant provided the following description of the Spanish behavior upon receiving some gold from a noble party representing the emperor at the entrance to the capital city:

And when they had given them the gift, they appeared to smile, to rejoice exceedingly and to take great pleasure. Like monkeys they seized upon the gold. It was as if they were satisfied, sated, and gladdened. For in truth they thirsted mightily for gold; they stuffed themselves with it, and starved and lusted for it like pigs.

THE MAN-EATING MYTH

And they went about moving the golden streamer back and forth, and showed it to one another, all the while babbling; and what they said was gibberish [Sahagun 1955: 31].

Although the narrator was alive at the time, it is unlikely he was present at the event, but he does portray the Aztec image of the Spaniards.

The Spaniards meanwhile were struck by the cultural level of the natives. The capital, Tenochtitlán, as well as other cities of the empire, was on a par with the major metropolises of Europe. Their size, population, architecture and cultural items and the order which prevailed were, in Cortés' words, "almost incredible." The situation was a classic instance of the confrontation between the civilized and barbarian. Only this time the latter had a superior military technology to match their aggressive intentions. Due to Montezuma's vacillation, the barbarians were soon inside the gates. An agreement was struck between the two, with the Aztecs recognizing the King of Spain as the overlord and Cortés as his representative in New Spain. However, after only six days in the city, Cortés wrote that, having seen something of its marvels, he felt that its ruler should no longer be "entirely free." Montezuma was persuaded to move to the Spaniards' quarters and submit to house arrest. This maneuver eventually led to a popular uprising and to the emperor's death.

The Aztec council reacted by electing Cuauhtemoc, a kinsman of Montezuma and a much more forceful character, to the throne. In this way, the revolt was brought under control and a war of resistance organized. Cortés and his men, laden with treasure, were forced to beat a hasty and disorganized retreat from the city with great loss of life in what came to be known as *La Noche Triste*. The Spaniards took refuge in the nearby city of Tlaxcala, which was both independent of and an enemy of the Aztecs. After a period of repair and preparations, the Spaniards and their Indian allies returned to Tenochtitlán. After a drawn-out siege, involving the display of some valor on both parts and significant death and suffering on the Aztec side, the city surrendered. The Spaniards now had their first colony on *Tierra Firma*. Despite their good intentions and belated attacks of Christian conscience, the Indians of Mexico were in for the same fate as those of the islands. A hundred years after Spanish contact and rule, and as the result of the war, lingering resistance, in some areas famine, and the imposition of a harsh colonial regime, but primarily due to the introduction of new diseases, the Indian population of the Valley of Mexico shrank from an estimated one and a half million to seventy thousand (Gibson 1964: 6). Thus the culmination of the clash between the two cultures, usually referred to as the Conquest, was also the almost complete obliteration of the indigenous inhabitants and their culture. The outcome of the adventure was akin to genocide, but the Spaniards were able to rationalize the deed. Sometime shortly after the Conquest, it became apparent that in addition to being idolaters the Aztecs were both sodomists and cannibals. By the twentieth century, Aztec cannibalism had become an ethnohistorical fact. The only question remaining for the present-day proselytizers for a theoretical persuasion—as opposed to the past proselytizers for a religious faith—is: how many were eaten and what is the "true" reason?

The type of analysis pursued here requires as far as possible the dismissal of prevailing notions and preconceived truths and conclusions while reconsidering the past of the New World. The obvious starting point for the Aztecs is with the work of Cortés, who, like Columbus in the Caribbean was not only present at the time but recorded his observations as the events unfolded. Lacking the complete picture made available by the passage of time, he was not as prone to legitimize the repercussions of his adventures, since they were not yet apparent. His observations were often just that, rather than a rendering or reorganization of past events which could rest more comfortably with the prevailing morality.

THE MAN-EATING MYTH

Cortés was an adventurer and gentleman freebooter almost until his death. As a consequence his literary remains are limited. The Cortésian account of the conquest of the New World is contained in the purest form in five long letters to King Charles of Spain. Written between 1519 and 1526, while Cortés was still in the midst of battlefield engagements, they read like the military dispatches they were intended to be.

There are various editions of these documents available. The version employed here contains no reference to the observation of cannibalism, but there are a few brief and explicable allusions to the topic as the situation between the Aztecs and Spaniards became more severe (Cortés 1962). First, as usual, there was some suspicion on the part of the Indians as to the nature of the Spaniards (Tapia 1963: 31). The possibility that the Europeans might be cannibals did not go unconsidered by the natives, but the outcome of the war ensured that this idea was not fully developed. The victors always claim the privilege of redefining the vanquished. If the latter's culture is partially obliterated, the task is even easier. In contrast, the initial Spanish suspicion that the Indians of the mainland were man-eaters like their island brothers has come down to us today as an unambiguous historical fact. However, this idea cannot be traced directly to Cortés, who was the initial chronicler of the era.

Upon entering the capital for the first time, Cortés explicitly forbade the practice of human sacrifice to the Aztec deities. This violation of Spanish civil and religious law meant that there is no mention of a single soul being sacrificed or eaten during the Spaniards' initial stay in the capital. Their expulsion a few months later and subsequent attack on the city changed this. At one of the many confrontations between Europeans and Indian, when the natives were given the opportunity to submit peacefully, Cortés reports a curious verbal exchange which took place. One of his officers shouted that if the Indians did not surrender the Spanish intended to maintain the siege until the Aztecs starved and eventually died of hunger. Not to be outdone in the war of words, an Aztec replied that they would never starve because when their supplies ran out they were going to eat the Spaniards and their Indian allies (Cortés 1962: 152). Cortés also mentions that one of his captains informed him that a group of captured Spaniards was offered to the Aztec gods, since at dusk their pale figures were seen ascending the great sacrificial pyramid of the city. There is no mention in this first observation of the event that these unfortunate victims were subsequently eaten (1962: 199). The most explicit reference to cannibalism is distilled from a letter by one of Cortés' officers who was operating independently of the main force. Cortés says in one of his dispatches that this officer, having put the Indians to rout, found among their supplies corn and "roasted babies" (1963: 107). Cortés does not confirm or elaborate on this statement, but as a military man it is likely that he realized the import this would have on the home front. Even in light of today's view of the Aztecs, this gruesome episode fails to fit their image. The report does confirm, though, that truth is often the first casualty of any war. The more savage the enemy is depicted as being the better, and what could be more despicable than military rations in the form of roasted babies?

A secondary account of the Conquest is available from Gómara, Cortés's personal secretary, who received five hundred ducats from the conquistador's family to provide a more readable and flamboyant account of the events. Naturally enough this version is much more colorful and dramatic, and the conquistador is depicted as a much more eloquent and heroic figure. Nevertheless, there is no claim that Cortés or his companions witnessed cannibalism. Again, the references to the topic are editorial and dramatic asides inserted by the biographer. Retelling the hero's experiences among the Cholulans, who were allies of the Aztecs, Gómara is able to read the Indian mind. When Cortés requested provisions for the last leg of the journey to the Aztec capital, Gómara says, these devious Cholulans "smiled and *said to themselves*" (italics added): "Why do these men want to eat, when they themselves will soon be eaten, served up with chili? Indeed, if Montezuma, who wants them for his own table, would not have been angry with us, we should have eaten them ourselves by this time" (127). In Gómara's version of the previously mentioned exchange of insults between opposing figures, the Aztec replies that the Spaniards are not fit food for humans, so instead their bodies are going to be sent to the royal zoo for the animals (209–10). The ritual murder of the captured Europeans on the pyramid is also included in the biography, but again there is no hint that they were food for man as well as the gods (281–82).

The reports of Alvarado (1963), which were written on the spot from outlying areas and then forwarded immediately to Cortés, also fail to mention cannibalism. In summary, those accounts composed at the time by participants in the expedition allude in a few possible instances to Aztec cannibalism, but make no claim to having observed such an act. In order to understand how the Aztecs were converted into the classic man-eaters they are today, it is only necessary to review the literary works of those conquistadors who penned their memoirs later in life. By then, they were different men, living in different times. The consequences of the Conquest were becoming a matter of some moral concern, and the fate of the Indians had become a matter of debate in the capitals of Europe. The Spaniards had by then won the war, but the rationale for conquest and the character of colonial rule were lively issues. Thus Francisco de Aguilar, one of Cortés's major lieutenants, wrote more than fifty years after his return to Spain that the Aztecs' captives were eaten as a "very tender delicacy" (1963: 164). The "Anonymous Conquistador," whose belated account may or may not be authentic, but either way is a reflection of the times, concludes his essay on the Conquest with a final acontextual paragraph which states that, in addition to being sodomites and excessive drinkers, the Aztecs went to war for the sake of human food (Anonymous Conquistador 1963: 181).

The most prolific scribe among the participants in the Conquest turned out to be Bernal Díaz (1970), an obscure military figure whose name fails to appear in the other accounts. He was moved to add his own reminiscences to the lists by the appearance of Gómara's slavish biography of Cortés. Díaz felt this popular document unfairly diminished the significance and accomplishments of other members of the expedition. He hoped to set the record straight in his "true account" of the subjugation of Mexico. In bits and pieces he ordered his recollections during his later years as a resident of colonial Guatemala (Cerwin 1963). In this particular saga of a youth spent in war, the anthropophagic character of the Indians begins to take a more vivid form. What were formerly intentions and fears now, with the passage of time, became actual deeds. Consequently, Díaz often mentions in passing that people were eaten; being threatened with this horrible fate himself; observing special places and instruments for this purpose; seeing captives and slaves being fattened for the cooking pot; and being informed that Montezuma only partook of the choicest thighs. The sacrifice of the captured Spaniards also makes an appearance in a more stirring way. In a remarkable visual feat, Díaz describes the "stone knives" used to remove the "palpitating hearts" of the naked victims. He adds to this that their bodies were then kicked down the pyramid to the base where they were butchered, since the flesh was later to be eaten, while the entrails were then fed to the zoo animals. The reader must empathize with the author, who concludes, "Thank God that they are not carrying me off to-day to be sacrificed" (Díaz 1970: 436). Even the most incredulous has to give way before this tableau until it is realized that the author does not claim to have seen anyone eaten. Instead, he depicts a colorful barbaric scenario which inevitably leads to the assumption that people were eventually eaten. However, this is not the same as having observed the act. Other historians and interpreters of the clash between Indian and European, to be discussed momentarily, who were neither alive at the time nor present at the events, fail to make this distinction between sacrifice and cannibalism. Their images of

THE MAN-EATING MYTH

what happened were not impinged upon by the actual experience, so that their commentary on a former cannibalism became even more exact and assured.

The adventurers who came to America were religious to the extent that they believed they were on a Christian mission. Undoubtedly this attitude accounted for some of their excesses, but at the same time these soldiers had a grudging admiration for Aztec culture and martial spirit. This was not to be the case for the next group of Spanish commentators, who represented a more dogmatic and formal religious viewpoint. The transformation of the Aztecs from civilized to barbarian was accomplished by the deft intellectual management of these friars. The compassion they often displayed for the Aztecs as human beings with a supernatural and natural capability equal to that of the European was matched by their virulent hatred of almost every aspect of Indian culture. In this respect, the friars were in direct opposition to the conquistadors, who often commented favorably on Aztec culture while eliminating its representatives; indeed, Cortés specifically commented on the piety of the Aztec priesthood in contrast to what he considered to be the venal life-style of certain Spanish religious orders.

The religious interpreters of the last days of Indian culture in the decades after pacification set out to reorder the record in a Christian perspective. Strangely enough, these very same individuals are today used as reliable sources for pre-contact Aztec culture, even though no group of specialists ever had a better reason or stronger desire to misinterpret and distort the material. Therefore it is not surprising that the limited documentation for Aztec cannibalism rests heavily on these sources, for this purported former vice regularly came in for strong denunciation. This condemnation was expressed within the context of an often deep understanding of Aztec culture, based upon ability in the native language and years of reflection. Yet the prose is always tinged by the inevitable dogmatic denunciation of native culture.

A basic source for sixteenth-century knowledge of Indian

customs, and therefore cannibalism, is the collected works of Durán (1964 and 1971), whose historical and ethnographic accomplishments are impressive. At the same time, this friar took pains to make explicit his feelings on the former barbarism of the natives. On the subject of their civilization he was of the opinion that the Indians "will never find God until the roots have been torn out, together with that which smacks of their ancestral religion" (1971: 54).

The author of this quotation was born in Spain in the decade after the conquest. When he was a young boy, his family migrated to Mexico, so Durán grew up in the former Aztec capital. In 1561, he was ordained as a Dominican priest and began his mission among the Indians and the study of their culture. In the process, he compiled three different manuscripts, *Book of the Gods and Rites, The Ancient Calendar* and *The Aztecs,* in that order. The folios circulated privately during the sixteenth century, were forgotten for some time and were finally published in the late nineteenth century. His accounts assume the prior existence of Aztec cannibalism as a correlative of human sacrifice. The vice is referred to a score of times in the text as evidence of the unworthiness of Aztec culture. There is more to the story as the mysterious thread of barbarism winds its way through the labyrinth of Durán's mind.

This attitude compels him to write, "I cannot help but believe that these Indians are the children of Israel" (1964: 6). In some ways, this was Durán's most reasonable hypothesis on the subject of the origin of Aztec culture. The vexing and, to the pious, even terrifying problem was the many parallels between Aztec and European religions, including Christianity. In his study of Aztec religion, Durán uncovered a set of moral injunctions similar to the Ten Commandments, mythical figures vaguely reminiscent of biblical heroes, and rites similar to those of the pre-covenant Israelites. This last category included the worship of idols and the sacrifice of children as recorded in the 105th Psalm: "the blood of their own sons and daughters, whom they sacrificed to the idols of Canaan." As a man of his times, Durán was also not beyond subscribing to the familiar sixteenth-century accusation that, like the Aztecs, the Jews of Europe engaged in ritual murder in order to acquire blood for the preparation of a sacred bread (Slutsky 1971). (The incredulous need only refer to manuscripts published during the period depicting both groups engaged in the practice; Kisch 1949.) A powerful enough idea generates its own evidence, and Durán was tormented by these echoes and reflections. He vacillated between the Judaic theme and the even more horrifying thought that the Indians might once have been converted to Christianity and in isolation lapsed into a former paganism.

As a scholar of both the Old and New Testaments, Durán knew that Christ had instructed his original disciples "to go and preach to all nations." The Aztecs also had a tradition of a great moral teacher and lawgiver by the name of Topiltzin, who had come from the east, whence he later returned. Durán felt this figure may have been the much-traveled apostle St. Thomas, who was supposed to have visited the Indies. This latter-day preacher of the faith was of the opinion that his more illustrious forerunner likely departed before completing his mission, since the Indians were rude, fickle and ignorant. Further, as Durán was so well aware, the Aztecs were inclined to believe in the most fabulous things "without any true basis or facts" (Durán 1971: 59–60). According to Durán's interpretation of the story, this figure also prophesied an eventual invasion by more strangers from the east who would avenge his poor reception and ill treatment at the hands of the Mexicans. Therefore, for Durán the Aztec destruction was inevitable and justified, but their conversion to the true faith was still to be achieved.

Last, Durán mulled over the most hideous alternative: that, instead of Moses or St. Thomas, Satan himself had been among the Aztecs and taught them a perversion of Christianity, which would also account for some of the confusing similarities. This nightmare was dismissed as Durán settled on the "Lost Tribe of

Israel" possibility and devoted a portion of his time and travels to trying to locate a Hebrew Bible in the Mesoamerican jungles. To be sure, his search eventually uncovered a picture book of the Aztec religion which had been saved from the earlier Spanish destruction of Indian documents as works of the devil. However, this and other manuscripts were unconvincing to Durán, who died without completely resolving the matter.

Amid these various discourses and reflections, Durán makes numerous references in his text to human sacrifice and cannibalism. Discussion of the latter is usually in the form of "the body was eaten" or "the body was taken away and eaten." Despite these comments, Durán never observed an instance of Aztec cannibalism, since the presumed custom had been abolished fifty years before. Nevertheless, he gave the idea a continued currency in a more scholarly context. Durán was one of a pair of ethnographically inclined monks who placed the stamp of authenticity on the previously unsubstantiated notion of Aztec cannibalism. His colleague in this affair was Fray Bernado de Sahagún, another highly touted figure when the subject of cannibalism is under analysis.

Sahagún did not suffer from Durán's more extreme historical delusions. Consequently his thirteen-volume record of Aztec history and culture and the Conquest, which has come down to us as *The Florentine Codex,* is an admirable scholarly feat. Like his predecessor, Sahagún took some pains to learn Aztec, and through the use of informants and a questionnaire systematically recorded numerous aspects of the traditional native culture. There is no doubt that Sahagún's intellectual accomplishments are many, and they are generally beyond reproach; but, like Durán, he reflected many attitudes of the day, inviting a consideration of the effect these social and intellectual features may have had on his interpretations and intentions.

His volumes clearly convey the impression that Sahagún had an intrinsic scholarly interest in Aztec society. Simultaneously they also show he believed the exercise was a necessary correlate to stamping out traditional Aztec cultural achievements for the sake of conversion. Therefore it is not surprising that the first volume, which introduces the reader to the Aztec gods, concludes with a sermon-like appendix denouncing and castigating the Indians for the errors of their ways. He adds that their conquest by the Spaniards was God-sent chastisement for the Aztec failure to immediately abandon their deities. He also announces that a certain pre-contact ritual of particular repugnance, which he referred to as "this great heresy and abominable sin," was still being observed in secret. The traditional act in question was the creation by the Aztec priests of dough images of their god which were distributed and eaten by those in attendance (Sahagún 1950: *passim*). This and similar occurrences had their effect on Sahagún's objectivity and are suggestive for a present-day evaluation of his contributions to the debate on cannibalism.

Sahagún was born in Spain, and arrived in Mexico after almost ten years of Spanish rule. Some time later, he initiated his monumental reconstruction of Aztec society and culture. His project included information on myth and folklore, as well as customs and history, and culminated in separate volumes devoted to a somewhat disparate subject matter ranging from *The Origin of the Gods* to *The Merchants* and *The Conquest of Mexico*. Each book was accompanied by illustrations drawn by the informants, who were alive during the pre-Conquest era and also provided the running commentary on the scenes depicted. Their remarks were recorded by Sahagún, who later reorganized and edited the material with the assistance of a number of his Indian former students who were conversant in Aztec, Spanish and Latin (Bandelier 1971). Even at this initial stage, the data were being filtered and interpreted by a number of separate minds. Further, according to present-day students (D'Olwer and Cline 1973) of the corpus and its author, Sahagún's objective was not absolute historical truth. Like contemporary ethnographers dealing with similar problems, Sahagún hoped to produce versions of the past which his informants believed were true. In the process he "evoked old concepts, couched often in highly symbolic terms, sometimes in obscure language" (D'Olwer and Cline 1973: 189). The significant point is that we are not dealing with a verbatim rendition of traditional culture, even if that were possible, but rather with a mosaic filled in by various artisans under the direction of a master craftsman who had a projected completed vision in mind.

These prefatory remarks are not designed to sabotage the material on cannibalism nor to disarm the reader, for it is surprising, in light of the reliance placed on this collection, that there is little reference to cannibalism *per se*. Specifically, only two of the thirteen volumes, *The Ceremonies* and *The Merchants*, contain fragmentary references to Aztecs eating human flesh. Further, these are not informants' admissions to having participated, nor are they eyewitness accounts. Instead, the narrators mention how the flesh of a sacrificial victim would be taken to the privacy of a merchant's home, priestly temple or noble palace, where it was "stewed" and eaten. In only one instance is anything approaching detail provided (1959: 67). The other references are the familiar "the body was taken away" or "the flesh was later eaten." The informants' idea that the elite are the consumers of human flesh is a common theme which we will encounter again in other cultural contexts. These comments provide a strange contrast to the description of other customs about which the informants are able to provide a seemingly endless amount of detail. This includes the portrayal of human sacrifice, which was a commonplace event among the Aztecs. It is easy to assume that human sacrifice is the same as, or leads to, cannibalism, but they are not one and the same. This is mentioned since the Aztec skull racks, sometimes casually referred to by other commentators as the evidence for Aztec cannibalism, indicate that many died; but they do not prove that any were eaten.

There are other references to the consumption of human flesh in the codices, but these are another matter. They do not add further support, but instead indicate that the available minimal evidence should be treated with some caution. A good example is an informant's statement that during an earlier reign there was a terrifying eclipse of the sun. At the time, it was said that "demons of darkness" would appear on earth and eat people (1954: 2). This suggests, among other things, that in Aztec mythology the consumption of human flesh was associated with the unknown, feared and evil, not the mundane everyday world of humans. The activities of these two spheres are normally kept separate in any cosmology. The mention of cannibalism in the contrasting contexts of good and evil, natural and supernatural, myth and reality is an ethnographic oddity.

Other references to cannibalism include Aztecs, but in these instances they are being eaten, rather than eating. According to the text, Aztec merchants often preceded the flag, and their incidental intelligence-gathering often aided in the subjugation of other areas. However, if they were caught spying, their fate was death and to be "served with chili sauce" (1950: 17–20). An implication of this reference is the barbarity of the non-Aztecs who would resort to such behavior. This is a most opportune moment to add that, of the hundreds and hundreds of pictographs contained in the Sahagún manuscripts, there is only a single illustration of cannibalism. One would expect that what today is assumed to have been a common occurrence would have more coverage. Yet all we have is this single picture, which portrays an unfortunate Aztec victim being eaten by an enemy. This event is discussed in *The Soothsayers* as an incidence of particularly bad fortune which could befall an Aztec warrior (1957: plate 31). Those so inclined could argue, if they wish, that this is merely an indication that all the Indians of Mexico were cannibals, but in addition to prejudgment, there are more subtle intellectual faults to such a conclusion.

Finally, there are the numerous references to the symbolic cannibalism, or Aztec communion, which was so disconcerting to Durán (Sahagún 1951, 1952 and 1953). In addition to preparing dough images of deities, the Aztecs also made similar representations of human sacrificial victims. In a statement bearing a close correspondence to the description of human cannibalism, but in this instance referring to the dough image, it is said: "They took it to their homes, [for] it was in truth their captive, and ate it. They offered it to their kin and to their neighbors who all ate of it" (1951: 135). In addition to arousing the ire of the Spaniards, this situation was ripe for misinterpretation. The line between a natural and a supernatural communion with the victim is not as obvious as we would like to believe. As we shall see, this sort of symbolism is, as often as not, misinterpreted in the literature on other cultures. The idea that others may have developed symbolic structures as subtle as our own is not easily accepted. In the case of the first missionaries to the New World, the idea was an affront to Christian dignity.

This is the most opportune point to leave Sahagún momentarily and skip ahead a few centuries to modern scholarship. This interlude is proposed in order to consider in their proper context Harner's musings on what he refers to as the "enigma" of Aztec cannibalism. As mentioned in the opening chapter, Harner (1977a) has accused his professional colleagues of diminishing the extent of Aztec human sacrifice. He proposes to set the record straight by returning to Cortés, Díaz, Sahagún and Durán as the basic sources. According to new estimates which he introduces, the standard figure of 15,000 human sacrifices annually must be dismissed, since according to Harner a quarter of a million souls in the Valley of Mexico actually met their ultimate fate in this manner. He shows himself to be something less than a perfectionist when it comes to statistical methods, since he arrives at this figure by multiplying the "thousands of temples" by "the estimated one to three thousand" sacrificed at each per year (1977a: 119).

According to his thesis, the lack of adequate domesticated animals in relation to the population size implied a protein deficiency which led to "large-scale cannibalism, disguised as sacrifice" (1977a: 118). One would imagine the Aztecs could have conceived of a better "cover" for the deed than public execution at the apex of a pyramid. Harner also makes the familiar but un-

demonstrated connection between human sacrifice and cannibalism. As reasonable as this may seem, one act was frequently
observed while the other never was. Be that as it may, this is only
one of many problems, since Harner relies upon *The Florentine
Codex*, which has many strong points, but, as demonstrated, these
do not include adequate documentation for cannibalism. Recognizing this minor flaw in his argument, Harner unabashedly
opines that Sahagún's Indian informants "probably took the
anthropophagic aspect for granted, and may have commonly
failed to mention its practice in their descriptions of the different
details of ceremonies and rites" (1977a: 125). In other words, in a
singular inversion of the scholarly method, the lack of documentation is actually offered as evidence for the existence of a
custom. Although a novel procedure, the technique is not entirely
convincing.

Equally important, damaging contradictory evidence from
Sahagún and other sources is ignored. Most pertinent were the
tribulations of the inhabitants of Tenochtitlán during the siege,
which made a lasting vivid impression on Indian and Spaniard
alike. Hearing that the civilian residents of the city were scav-
enging for food at night, Cortés, his biographer reports, rode into
the city and "slaughtered many of them, mostly women and
children and unarmed men" (Gómara 1964: 287). He also reports
that after the siege, heaps of dead bodies were a common sight and
those Indians still alive were so emaciated that the victorious
Spaniards were actually filled with pity (288). This was also
confirmed by one of Sahagún's informants, who recounts with
greater detail and sympathy:

"And all the commonfolk suffered torments of famine.
Many died of hunger. . . . And all was eaten—lizards and
swallows; and maize straw, and salt grass. And they ate
colorin wood, and they ate the glue orchid, and the frilled
flower; and tanned hides, and buckskin, which they roasted,
baked, toasted, or burned, so that they could eat them; and
they gnawed sedum and mud brick. Never had there been

such suffering. It was terrifying how they were besieged; truly in great numbers they starved" [Sahagun 1955: 100–101].

The fact that the Aztecs did not take advantage of what should have been a bonanza disturbed some of the commentators. Gómara lacked the modern terminology, but in essence concluded that the Aztecs must have been exocannibals; otherwise they would not have "died of starvation" (1964: 293). To an early twentieth-century student of anthropology (Loeb 1964) this anomalous situation meant that the Aztecs only ate human flesh as a ritual, while preferring death from starvation if the flesh was not properly consecrated. Frankly, these explanations are logical possibilities, but this suffering without resorting to cannibalism seriously undermines Harner's nutritional hypothesis. If people were food to the Aztecs, then the siege should have been a time of plenty for the survivors. The only convenient course of action for an ecologically oriented theorist is to ignore such information. Harner's literary gap also includes an account written by a group of anonymous Aztec survivors who penned their reminiscences seven years after the Conquest. Their version details the suffering of the city dwellers, but again there is no mention of cannibalism being resorted to during the siege. As some indication that this is not a "cover-up," it may be noted that although the authors of the text admit to the sacrifice of Spanish captives, there is not a hint that victims served as a meal for the starving Indians (Leon-Portilla 1962: 127–49).

The Spanish victory put an official end to human sacrifice and presumed cannibalism, and Harner concludes that the introduction of domesticated animals from Europe permitted the Indians to abandon their old ways (1977a: 123). This explanation runs counter to the tenor of his argument, since if the consumption of human flesh was caused by overpopulation, then the demise of the practice would more likely be the result of the drastic numerical decrease caused by the Conquest. Harner's explanation, however, does provide an unwitting moral and ecological justification for the Spanish colonization of Mexico—though it provides little else. His re-examination of the basic sources which were supposed to set the record straight has only obscured matters. To paraphrase a favorite expression of one of those involved, Harner has created something of a tempest in the cannibal pot by bringing back to life those colleagues he accused of covering up the facts. However, the first response was favorable; Harris, as Harner's mentor and theoretical compatriot, lauded his former protégé's "intelligence and courage . . . for solving the riddle of Aztec sacrifice" (1977: 108). Others might justly claim Harner has created the riddle, but they will have to wait their turn. In a collection of popular essays on the origins of culture with the catchy title *Cannibals and Kings* Harris concludes his selection on the pre-contact states of Mesoamerica by informing his readers that the term "high-civilization" is a "wildly inappropriate" characterization of the Aztec state (95). With this conscious misuse of a technical phrase having no relation to value-laden moral standards, he invites the audience to consider his next essay, "The Cannibal Kingdom."

Harris initiates this discussion by boldly stating that "nowhere else in the world had there developed a state sponsored religion . . . so thoroughly dominated by violence, decay, death and disease" (99), and refers to the Aztec priesthood as "ritual slaughterers in a state sponsored system geared to the production and distribution of substantial amounts of animal protein in the form of human flesh" (109). He supports these contentions, which could have been penned by a sixteenth-century cleric, by co-opting Harner's basic premises on protein deficiency interspersed with some asides on the similar practices of the Tupinamba and Huron and judicious quotations from what he defines as the "eye-witness accounts" of the conquistadors Cortés and Díaz. Like Harner, he mistakenly assumes that large-scale human sacrifice inevitably results in an equally grand cannibalistic appetite; but others with less of a personal stake in the matter have been more critical of Harner's solution to his problem.

THE CLASSIC MAN-EATERS   73

The first serious appraisal of Harner's argument was presented by a non-anthropologist (Montellano 1978), who offers the reasonable but also embarrassing reminder to his anthropological colleague that to assume, as does Harner, that a diet requires domesticated animal protein is "quite ethnocentric," since it is based upon the European experience. Furthermore, he argues that some of the malnutrition suffered by the Indians of Mesoamerica can actually be attributed to the substitution of European foodstuffs for the traditional dietary items. Montellano then goes on to list the various sources of wild and domestic vegetable proteins which provided a sufficient dietary base during the pre-Columbian era. Interestingly enough, he informs us that amaranth, which was a staple grain and major source of protein for the Aztecs, was banned as a cultivated crop by the Spaniards, since it was closely associated with the natives' traditional religious rituals referred to in the previous pages. Finally, he mentions that Harner fails to consider the vast amounts of foodstuffs funneled into the Aztec empire as tribute from subservient neighbors, which was brought to a halt by the Conquest. In short, his argument denies on various grounds the notion of the existence of a protein deficiency and allows the reader to conclude that if ever there was one, it was caused by the Spaniards, whose invasion seriously dislocated the pre-existing economy and ecology of Central Mexico. Although the author accepts without comment the former existence of Aztec cannibalism, he suggests there must have been religious motivation, since the available evidence does not permit the assumption of a scarcity of protein.

The second rejoinder in this latter-day debate on Aztec morality has been offered by another student of the area (Price: 1978), who, like Harner and Harris, claims the label of cultural materialist. Possibly as the result of a desire to show a greater degree of materialistic scientific sophistication than her adversary, for stylistic reasons Price's argument is more difficult to follow. In her opening remarks, she claims that Harner's argument "poses serious substantive, interpretative and epistemological prob-

THE MAN-EATING MYTH

lems . . . which are exacerbated, furthermore, by the extension of a hypothesis to explain the patterning of state-organized warfare, imperial expansion and demographic strategy" (98). After characterizing Harner's essay as "opaque," the author claims to be in possession of a still-secret but nonetheless "more powerful explanatory model" to explain away Aztec cannibalism. This model seems to have some bearing on the attempt to stabilize the then-existing stratification and political systems, but she remarks that explication is beyond the scope of her present article (105). In a vocabulary of the devotees of a privileged persuasion, she lashes out at Harner for various "emic" and "etic" heretical lapses. With respect to my present purposes, her own marshaling of the evidence, like that of the more modest and readable Montellano, leads her to conclude that there are serious grounds to question the notion that the Aztecs suffered from a severe protein deficiency.

Oddly enough, throughout her diatribe Price frequently cites the contributions of none other than the previously mentioned Harris to demonstrate the error of Harner's ways. She even goes so far as to "especially thank" Harris for the germ of her argument and the stimulus to develop it (114). This is all rather interesting, but confusing for the outsider trying to follow the development of an academic controversy. However, the academic alliance situation does not detract from the main thrust of the rejoinders, which strongly suggest that Harner is on rather shaky grounds in his attempt to solve the problem he has created. None of those directly involved in print has yet to consider that it is impossible to adequately account for a practice which has not been demonstrated to have existed. Sahagún's theological explanations for cannibalism, which led us into this digression, may not be as fashionable today among scholars, but his account deserves the more serious attention, so a return to the sixteenth century is ordained.

An adequate evaluation of his work calls for some appreciation of the intellectual climate of the period. It is particularly significant that the collection and recording of native customs, especially in the local language, was a delicate and even dangerous matter for ethnographers such as Durán and Sahagún. At times the manuscripts which resulted were banned as being a danger to true conversion and even possibly heretical. Consequently the accounts which eventually saw the light of day were carefully scrutinized by a number of secular and religious offices, including the Inquisition (D'Olwer and Cline 1973). Serious attention to the matter of native culture was cause enough for alarm. However, the obvious similarities between Aztec religion and Christianity in the form of rituals and associated beliefs was the more sensitive area. For this reason, Sahagún had to be constantly on guard. This is expressed in his appendix to the first volume, where he instructed natives who were aware of this continued idolatry to immediately inform the "justice of the Holy Church" (1950: 45).

It would be odd indeed if this atmosphere did not taint the reporting of Aztec culture or failed to render the natives more barbaric in terms of European standards than the material permitted. There have been greater excesses in the name of religion than ethnographic embellishment, allowing us to assume that such deformation is not beyond the realm of possibility. The translator of one edition of the *Codex* reports that chauvinism played its potential role in the account of the Conquest. According to Bandelier (1971), the authorities made Sahagún omit certain "facts" and change his narration of certain events. Sahagún circumvented these directions by retaining the original account in the accompanying text in the Aztec tongue for future translators. Finally, the history of the *Codex* is a complex affair in itself. The sequence of events includes the disappearance of the first version, the second, sanitized version and then a third version prepared under the author's supervision. The potential for editorial pollution as a consequence of the numerous minds and hands engaged in producing the version we have today must also be recognized.

A thoughtful evaluation of the *Florentine Codex*, as well as allied primary sources, indicates some of the problems involved in assuming the anthropophagic nature of the Aztecs. The sound scholarly foundation so often assumed or alluded to evaporates upon investigation. This does not prove that the Aztecs did not consume human flesh in private rituals; nor does it demonstrate that they did not engage in this practice on a massive scale as a result of protein deficiency. What can be put forward with some assurance is the proposition that the evidence is too sparse, too ephemeral and too suspect on various grounds to suggest a positive assertion on this question. What can be demonstrated with no equivocation is the way in which the Aztec reputation for cannibalism has solidified over time and been used to denigrate this people's moral standards and cultural achievements. In a fascinating historical study of the Aztec image in western arts and letters, Keen (1971) has shown how their image has vacillated between one of mindless barbarism and one of noble savagery. However, through it all they have always remained cannibals. Sometimes they were denounced, at other times excused, for this deed. The Aztecs have weighed heavily on the European conscience. The mere existence of such an advanced civilization in the New World was bothersome, while its destruction is still a matter of some guilt to the collective intellectual conscience. As a result, cannibalism has always been a key element in any subsequent interpretation and commentary on the Conquest.

The immediate post-Conquest years demanded the strongest rationale and therefore the severest debasement of Aztec culture. D'Anghera (1912), mentioned earlier as the harvester of tales from returning Spaniards, opened his discussion of the Aztecs by informing the reader that they practiced both cannibalism and sodomy, had no laws and went naked. In the symbolic context of both the sixteenth and twentieth centuries, D'Anghera was implying, in total disregard of the facts, that they did not possess culture. Moreover, he argued, they lacked the intelligence of normal humans and were incapable of improving on their own lot (1912: 274–75). This implied both that the Aztecs deserved their conquest and that the Spaniards were justified in imposing a colonial regime.

The "true" nature of the Aztecs was of more than passing interest in Christendom. Consequently a formal debate was arranged in Spain to determine whether, in accordance with Aristotle's argument, the Indians were a latter-day instance of "natural slaves." In what a perceptive historian of the era characterized as one of the most curious intellectual episodes of European history, the most learned figures of the nation debated and sat in judgment on the question of whether the Indians of the New World were "Dirty Dogs" or "Noble Savages" (Hanke 1974: 9). The notion of cannibalism figured in the arguments of both sides. The anti-Indian faction interpreted the custom as an aspect of the debased rude nature of the aborigines, who engaged in the act out of their natural perversity. In total ignorance of the realities of war and conquest, one major figure argued that, since twenty thousand had been sacrificed annually by the Aztecs, the thirty years of Spanish rule had saved 600,000 lives. The pro-Indian forces saw the act as a misguided ritual of respect for the dead which the true faith could easily build upon. According to Las Casas (1974), the Indians were on the right track, but just needed further spiritual guidance. Their other achievements, he felt, showed they had a moral capability equal to that of the European world. The eventual decision, arising from the great debate, to impose humanitarian limits on the character of colonial rule was academic. In New Spain, there was no equivocation, and those on the spot ruled the Indians with little regard for directives from the mother country. They took even less notice of the debates among learned monks in Latin.

The subsequent interpretations of Aztec culture have been less dramatic than the great debates of the sixteenth century. A nineteenth-century translator of Díaz asks the reader to excuse the excesses of the Spanish by bearing in mind the "revolting abominations" practiced by the natives (Lockhart 1884: vi). Victorian sensibilities apparently prevented him from mentioning the usual

THE MAN-EATING MYTH

"cannibalism and sodomy." Prescott, who demonstrates his richly deserved reputation as a historian of the Conquest, nonetheless comments on the Aztec "brutish appetite" for human flesh, which had a "fatal influence" on the empire (1909: 57). Ignoring the Spaniards' appetite for gold, he seems to imply that they actually went to war to stop the Aztecs from eating human flesh. He asserts: "The debasing institutions of the Aztecs furnish the best apology for their conquest" (57). In the same vein, Soustelle, the French interpreter of the era, refers to human sacrifice as the great gulf between Mexican and Spaniard (1962: 98). Finally, the most recent translator of Díaz points out that the Aztec fate at the hands of the Spaniards was "human" in comparison to what "other tribes of their own race or religion" might have meted out to the vanquished (Leonard 1970: 467).

The gradual transformation of what little evidence is available for Aztec cannibalism is also an indication of the continual need to legitimize the Conquest. Vaillant's highly regarded modern history of the Aztecs converts the illustration in *The Florentine Codex* mentioned before—of an Aztec being eaten by an enemy—into a picture with the caption "Aztec ritual of cannibalism" (Vaillant 1965: Plate 61). Granted this is one possible way of describing the event; but it clearly implies that the Aztec is the diner, rather than the dinner. Prescott provides a fanciful embellishment of Sahagún's limited remarks with the description of cannibalism as "a banquet teeming with delicious beverages and delicate viands, prepared with art and attended by both sexes" (1909: 53). The prose is such as to make one almost wish he was there, but not so for the author of a recent textbook, who describes the scene as an "intoxicated orgy of cannibalism" at the base of the pyramid used to sacrifice the victims (Pearson 1974: 504). The lack of evidence permits the portrayal of the scene according to the peculiar fancy of the author. However, for an anthropologist, one of the most depressing aspects of the process is the gradual degeneration of ethnographic standards. It would be gratifying to be able to think that the discipline becomes more "scientific"

Pictograph from *The Florentine Codex* of Sahagún, showing a captured Aztec being cooked by his enemies; sometimes referred to as evidence for Aztec cannibalism.

with time, but a review of the literature implies that such an assumption is unwarranted.

Nothing can be done for the Aztecs at this time. They no longer are. Their rapid demise necessitated the importation of slaves from Africa. Keen (1971: 89) reports that at the end of the sixteenth century a history of New Spain by a settler asked why no one pleaded for an abolition of the Negro slave trade. However, he was of the opinion that, although the Africans were also cannibals, they were somewhat superior to the Indians, since they did not sacrifice their victim first. Thus, as one group of cannibals disappeared, the European mind conveniently invented another which would have to be saved from itself by Europeans before it was too late.

THE
CONTEMPORARY
MAN — EATERS

The two cases examined in the previous chapter provide in our age meaningful reflections on the achievements of western civilization. One implication that can be drawn from the Conquest era is that our culture's intervention in the New World rendered a time and place habitable for civilized human beings. As a consequence, the descendants of this humanizing mission now occupy a corner of the world once the preserve of man-eaters. The two culture areas to be considered in this chapter have a more current significance.

Africa served as the most meaningful fringe of western civilization in the nineteenth century, while New Guinea has a similar function for our times. The mere mention of the two areas immediately conjures up certain popular images and impressions of the contest between civilization and its opposite. Consequently this survey reflects on a more contemporary moral philosophy, historical interpretation and science. We would like to believe that these intellectual activities, especially the last one, are as value-free as possible. Yet the idea of cannibalism continues to weave its way through these contemporary discourses. The message embodied just below the surface is also often little different from that propounded by sixteenth-century conquistadors and friars.

A classic dissection of one such corpus of cannibal literature for a particular area of Africa was carried out by Sir Edward Evans-Pritchard (1965). The autopsy was conducted with such deft elegance and precision, based upon the all-too-rare marriage of common and intellectual sense, that it provides the only fit entry point for an excursion into a land which for various reasons was once imagined to be the Dark Continent.

Evans-Pritchard managed to complete an extended period of

field research between 1927 and 1930 among the Azande of Central Africa without any untoward incidents. These very same people had an established reputation among other Sudanese groups as cannibals, and this notion had been substantiated in the dozens of books by Europeans which commented either in detail or in passing on the Azande appetite for human meat. In his careful scrutiny of his predecessors' literary efforts, Evans-Pritchard demonstrates that most of these avowals of Azande cannibalism are easily dismissed, due to the brevity of the author's stay in Azandeland or linguistic incompetence. He points out that (as in other instances examined above) some of the hearsay evidence is contained in the form of conversations between explorers and natives. This means either that the visitors learned the Azande tongue rapidly or that there were some Azande who spoke English, German or Italian—an even more unlikely possibility. In other instances, he notes that a number of the reporters never even passed through Azande country. The human failing which emerges most clearly from the morass of data is once again European plagiarism, rather than Azande cannibalism.

It would be misleading not to mention that Evans-Pritchard is of the opinion that there must have been some former cannibalism in the area because "there is no smoke without fire" (153). Still, this impression is tempered by his assessment that most often cannibalism was supposed to have been practiced by foreign elements which had been only partially assimilated into the Azande state. This syndrome of "others but not us" is a familiar one and will be considered in due course.

Some of the other commentaries on African groups are trifling, but almost always amusing. One traveler was told by the Arabs that many of the Congolese groups whom they formerly took as slaves deserved this fate, since they were cannibals. The European explorer was able to confirm this when he later passed among them and noticed their filed teeth. He assumed there could be but one reason for this. Being an optimist, though, he was sure that "white men of upright character" would soon "put an end to this" (Ward 1890: 163). Another "Congo hand" of the era was not convinced that this would happen, since he thought that the minimal European presence had allowed Africans to move about more than they had prior to European rule, and they had innocently picked up this bad habit from others. Prior to the arrival of civilization, he argued, African travelers had been eaten, so the idea could not have spread (Hinde 1897: 66). Moving to West Africa, we learn from *The Tailed Head-Hunters of Nigeria* that the people the author lived among did not indulge in cannibalism. However, he was informed that their neighbors to the south were not as squeamish, so he paid them a visit. Much to his disappointment, they refused to admit to the deed. Undaunted by this uncooperative behavior, he writes:

I asked them the reason why they pretended that they had given up the practice. . . . They would not tell me, saying that they did not like human flesh, but when I showed them my white arm, they admitted it might be better than chicken . . . [Tremearne 1912: 181].

Another anthropologist who has reviewed this sort of literature for Africa on similar topics bluntly concludes that these colorful accounts are more in the realm of slander than scholarship (George 1968: 185). In a similar tone, David Livingstone considered the evidence for cannibalism among an African group he was familiar with, and concluded with the terse comment: "A Scotch jury would say, Not Proven" (1874: 98). Since Livingstone spent a good portion of his adult life in East and Central Africa ministering to what he considered to be the spiritual and physical well-being of the natives he lived and died among, his experienced testimony should be of some value. However, those who followed in his footsteps in their rapid travels through the continent, such as the writers cited above, have felt the need to provide their readers with more sensational accounts of savagery.

Typical of the latter was Henry Morton Stanley, whose name is inextricably linked with that of his renowned predecessor.

Although both were classic romantic figures of their day, no two men could have been more dissimilar in so many other ways. Livingstone, by all accounts, was universally accepted by the Africans he encountered and went about his mission in tranquility. The experience of his would-be rescuer, Stanley, was another matter entirely. His own reports portray him as constantly set upon, in the very same areas traversed peacefully by Livingstone, by the most bellicose and savage people, whom he was forced to dispatch and rout with regularity. According to Stanley, these groups were more often than not also cannibals, intent upon the delicacy of the great white explorer. Thus in *Through the Dark Continent* we read that he had two cannibal guides; immediately consigned two of his dead porters to the swift river, lest they become food for the cannibals of the region; captured three cannibals in another area who, his guides said, smelled from the odor of human meat; and also was set upon by another group, shouting in an unknown dialect that they were going to eat Stanley and his party (Stanley 1878: *passim*). As usual, he did not observe cannibals in the act, but relied primarily for his information on the word of Arab slavers in the area, who had a vested economic interest in discouraging European encroachment in their preserves, since it posed a threat to the lucrative trade in human beings. Showing no favorites on this score, the Arabs also spread the word among the local groups that Stanley and his men were cannibals, which might explain to some extent his often harsh reception during his adventures.

It would be easy enough to continue to present some of the patently absurd evidence for African cannibalism in this fashion and conclude, like Livingstone, that nothing has been proved. However, this would undoubtedly encourage lingering suspicions about the existence of more reliable material. Further, the discussion so far may be amusing, but it is not instructive in the sense of manifesting how the idea of African cannibalism could

Illustration of nineteenth-century African cannibalism.

Further graphic evidence of African cannibalism.

become so widespread. Many would legitimately maintain, like one of the great figures of modern social anthropology, that where there is smoke there must be fire. However, the fact of the matter is that, despite the vastness of the continent, there are rather slim pickings. The best example of purported African man-eating for which there is more than a single account is provided by a work that the most recent commentator has titled *Cannibals and Tongo Players of Sierra Leone* (Kalous 1974). This material pales by comparison with the extent and significance of the Aztec data, but the instance is the best that can be managed. On the brighter side, this case study does reveal the intellectual processes involved in the propagation of the notion of African cannibalism and the way it is maintained in our own time.

An idea is able to gain and retain the aura of essential truth through telling and retelling. This process endows a cherished notion with more veracity than a library of facts. As the Aztec material so well demonstrates, documentation plays only a small role in contrast to the act of reconfirmation by each generation of scholars. In addition, the further removed one gets from the period in question, the greater is the strength of the conviction. Initial incredulousness is soon converted into belief in a probability and eventually smug assurance. The assumption of African cannibalism therefore is at a temporal crossroads. The vague notion and dispersed references are prevalent, but the enshrinement requires contemporary legitimization. This is provided in classic form by Kalous (1974), who recently felt compelled to rescue some of the data on African cannibalism from obscurity.

Kalous is of the opinion that through a misguided paternalism many European commentators have glossed over some of the more unpleasant aspects of African cultures, such as human sacrifice and cannibalism. Those anthropologists who have mentioned these and other unpleasantries have in a neutral tone dismissed them as functional adaptations. The result, he argues, is "a falsely positive, and positively false" portrait of pre-colonial Africa. His book is intended to show that British colonialism was a "positive and beneficial" experience for the ordinary African. This thesis is illustrated by his examination of cannibalism, a "starkly brutal aspect of African past [sic]" (1974: ix-x). The author hopes to demonstrate the validity of his claim by presenting without commentary the files relating to an outbreak of this activity from the colonial archives for the Sherbo district of Sierra Leone.

Some of the verbatim transcripts in Kalous's volume are taken from the communiqués of colonial figures who report on "the occasional murders to gratify an unnatural craving" (22) and say that "cannibalism has been in vogue for some time" (38) and the expected "I explained to them the evils of cannibalism . . ." (73). These are not meant to be the most incriminating comments, since they are the product of European outsiders. The testimony of Africans themselves on the subject is clearly intended to be the more significant confirmation of these dark deeds. In short order, we hear, in the words of unnamed Africans, the succinct "I ate some of the boy's flesh" (89); the exculpatory "My sister's daughter was the first victim, we eat . . . all of her. . . . We have no real reason for doing this, if bad people are born into this world they cannot help it . . ." (89); the explanatory "each member who receives a share is bound to supply another victim to be killed . . . the members eat their shares. The person is only killed for the purpose of being eaten" (104); and finally the conformatory "They offered me some flesh. . . . I declined to eat at first but when I saw how many they were I eat . . ." (199). What could be more persuasive than the self-incriminating remarks of the cannibals themselves? However, the contextual detail of these confessions indicates that some caution is called for, even in this apparently open-and-shut case. As mentioned, Kalous presents the documents without commentary, so that judgment requires further elucidation by other authorities.

In a recent history of Sierra Leone, Fyfe (1962: 442) refers in passing to the rumors of cannibalistic outbreaks that often circulated during the eighteenth and nineteenth centuries. These were received with some skepticism by the European authorities, since according to the Africans the cannibals transformed themselves into animals in order to carry out the deeds. In fact the government prevented the punishment of the accused man-eaters by local native rulers, since the grounds were frivolous. Fyfe's two brief allusions to cannibals in this context are an example of the suppression of negative detail which Kalous finds so unacceptable. However, examination of further information on this particular instance casts doubt on what would seem to be a fairly secure case of self-admitted cannibalism.

An earlier commentator (Alldridge 1901), with a lifetime of experience in this West African colony, reports that if a local death was thought to have been murder for the sake of cannibalism, the chief might call in the feared Tongo Players. These infamous detectors of evil were handsomely paid for their services from the fines which were levied against suspected leopard, baboon and alligator men who were thought to kill and then eat their victims. The Tongo Players' methods of detection were varied, but always lacking in subtlety and scientific method. One procedure forced suspects to remove a piece of hot iron from the bottom of a cauldron of boiling oil. If the hand was injured, then the alleged was assumed to be guilty and subsequently burned alive. A slightly more direct method involved an audience-participation play put on by the Tongo company. In this instance, summary justice was administered as guilty members of the audience were abruptly hit over the head by the Tongo actors and immediately thrown into a roaring fire (Alldridge 1901: 157–58). Another early figure on the scene (Beatty 1915) recounts various other actions of this type by Tongo Players, such as the immolation of eighty suspects in a single area, including one of the chiefs who had invited these specialists into his domain. Alldridge and Beatty considered the suppression of the Tongo Players' "regime of terror" based upon the native belief in and allegations of cannibalism as one of the most beneficial accomplishments of the colonial administration. This did not come soon enough for the victims or the survivors, whose accounts also litter Kalous's compendium. Those in the latter category may have escaped the ultimate fate, but their property was confiscated as payment of the enormous fines levied against the victims and their families. These survivors also mention how under torture they admitted to cannibalism, the ability to turn themselves into animals at will, and the possession of other magical powers.

A number of additional points and further comments are needed to complete the picture. First, it is obvious that these particular groups in Sierra Leone believe that cannibals exist as organized confraternities of evil. On this score, they are no different from many other African societies. The particular image of evil in the form of were-men is a common mental phenomenon for Africa (Joset 1955) and other world areas, including our own (Lindskog 1954). Second, many of the acts contained in the evidence or confessions are beyond human capability. Human beings, including those in Africa, cannot change themselves into animals—whether or not they claim to have done so, as in the case of some of the witnesses in Kalous's volume. This may be obvious to us, but even Europeans in close contact with the nightmare of another world appear to lose their normal perspective. A district commissioner in Sierra Leone filed a report on the alligator society which, sometime around the turn of this century, apparently was in possession of a submarine. The craft was thought to be made out of two canoes placed one on top of the other, providing room enough inside for a crew of man-eaters. In this fashion, they plied the river bottom before dragging down an unsuspecting victim and pulling him into the compartment through a hinged portal. With an air of *sangfroid* (often the most sought-after personality quirk of future British colonial officials) the author of the report concludes: "How air is supplied, or how the hinged door can be opened or closed when the canoe is under water, I cannot attempt to explain. That must be done by one who has been there. . . . The canoe is called *Koonkoo-bery* . . ." (Kalous 1974: 73). A more credulous reporter of this same phenomenon suggested that maybe the area between the two canoes was a sufficient air space (Berry 1912).

The material also indicates that cannibalism, if it existed outside the realm of suspicion and false accusation, would not have been condoned. In fact, people were executed because they were thought to be cannibals, or because it was convenient to think of them as such. In short, even according to this evidence cannibalism was not a custom in Africa but rather was viewed as a possible capital crime resorted to by criminals. An anthropologist who carried out research in Sierra Leone among the Mende reports that the idea of cannibals roving the night is still prevalent. The Mende believe that anyone who gains power over others achieves this by concocting and using a magical substance made from human fat. Such behavior is of course thought to be antisocial, to say the least, so political leaders are often accused of this sort of sorcery (Little 1967: 232–33). This last factor leads directly to the final consideration. The cannibal and Tongo Player drama acted out in Sierra Leone is an instance of the common phenomenon anthropologists refer to as an *anti-witchcraft movement*.

Like other instances of this phenomenon, the anti-witchcraft movement in traditional Africa had a wide distribution. This type of social movement also had its expression in medieval and later Europe and then, in colonial New England. These outbreaks of a perverted sense of morality had profound consequences which continue to figure heavily in our historical consciousness. There are a number of generic configurations in all instances, but those of most relevance here are the political implications. These movements to restore the moral order which is thought to be under attack arise in times of crises which may be brought on by any number of forces, ranging from economic distress to national disaster. In these moments of community crisis, witch-finders either emerge internally or, more often, are brought in to ferret out the human agents thought to be responsible for the problems. More likely than not, this situation sets in motion a political struggle between community factions who find the setting perfect for the resolution of unsettled matters. The reports involving the Tongo Players imply that the local men of influence dabbled in this dangerous competitive art. In one instance, one half of the chiefs of a single territory lost their lives in the ensuing struggle. These bouts, therefore, culminate in an alteration of political arrangements as certain prominent figures stand condemned of witchcraft and suffer the consequences. In Africa, this normally involved a fall from power or banishment, and only rarely death. In certain cultural systems, such as those of Sierra Leone and other African examples, cannibalism was thought to be a further heinous crime of the accused, and execution followed. However, rather than being an actual deed, cannibalism existed as an aspect of political ideology, and was employed in the process of attempting to discredit a political rival. Instructive instances of this sort of situation, with illuminating substantive parallels, are provided by the witch craze and anti-witchcraft movements which swept across Europe between the fourteenth and sixteenth centuries.

There is a vast literature on this bizarre historical incident, but none more enlightening than Trevor-Roper's (1969) succinct overview of an era which saw untold thousands burned at the stake for possessing evil supernatural abilities. The particular value of this study lies in its subtle appreciation of social currents and Trevor-Roper's sensitive examination of those ideas and actions which reflect so ingloriously on some of the most cherished institutions of western civilization. As he retells the story, the civil authorities either voluntarily or through external pressure called in those ecclesiastics with the special knowledge and ability to recognize witches. In time, representatives of both the rich and the poor, the powerful and the impotent, the despised and formerly respected found themselves staring down into the flames which were about to purify their mortal remains. Political scores were settled as some careers came to an end and others soared. In addition, the families of the accused paid fines and suffered confiscation of property which had accumulated as the result of the evil abilities possessed by the former owner. Confessions were extracted through the use of torture, as normal individuals admitted to fantastic powers and unspeakable crimes. This particular reign of terror was on a scale which dwarfed similar outbreaks in Sierra Leone.

The facts are commonplace, and there is general agreement that this was a lamentable period of European history. Less well known today is the function of the cannibalism theme, which played an important part in the medieval definition of malevolence. Surprisingly, this trait was believed to characterize the behavior of witches, satanists, heretics and at times the Jews. Some of the accused admitted to these crimes under torture, including having provided their own children for cannibalistic feasts (Parrinder 1963 and Murray 1970). The concordance between colonial Africa and the European Middle Ages is striking because the same symbols of homicide and cannibalism are used in the attempt to conceive of the ultimate in human depravity. The clerics of the European Inquisition are recast as the Tongo Players in Africa, but in both scenarios the victims are the same confraternity of witches with cannibalistic urges. The major difference in contemporary interpretations of these instances is that, in spite of similar evidence, there are no claims that thousands of Europeans in former times were cannibals. Instead, those who defined and persecuted the people accused of cannibalism now come in for moral and intellectual condemnation. In Africa, by contrast, the cannibalism is decried, and the colonial regime, for all its faults, is seen as a harbinger of better times.

Little need be added to this discussion of African cannibalism. The notion of anthropophagy on this continent is widespread, but it is difficult to isolate an instance worthy of detailed investigation. This lack of hard and fast historical evidence enshrined as both esoteric and common knowledge may have something to do with the fact that Africans and their traditional cultures are still with us. The effective colonial period in Africa usually spanned little more than fifty years. For all practical purposes, for most of the continent the era included only the years between the end of World War I and the 1960s as the decade of independence. Further, the colonial pressure was uneven. In some areas the European impact was next to negligible. There are no cultures in contemporary Africa which condone cannibalism as public custom or ritual, so we can safely assume there were none at the turn of the century. Those who believe that a few decades of ineffective European rule by a relative handful of administrators and missionaries were sufficient to eradicate what they assume was an ingrained custom know little about the continent beyond the cultural material contained in popular films. Those who would counter that ritual cannibalism was and is a feature of secret societies would do best to consider what kind of secret this would be if everyone was aware of the practice. The fact of the matter is that the notion of African cannibalism is just that.

The African case study closely corresponds to the Caribbean example, since the evidence is almost non-existent or easily dismissed. The next instance of purported anthropophagy conforms in some respects to the Aztec situation. Cannibalism in this case is assumed to be an extant custom and is commented on by modern social anthropology; but it also has implications for the most up-to-date medical theories. Caution is again called for. The evidence must be sifted with some care, and an open mind is still essential.

A discussion of infamous anthropophagists would be incomplete without considering the material from the highlands of New Guinea, anthropology's last remaining laboratory of classic primitives. Until contact with beings in outer space, New Guinea will have to serve as the cultural frontier of western civilization. The near-naked warrior with a stone axe over one shoulder and a pig bone through the nose, peering up at the vapor trails of his more advanced colleagues' latest weapon, is a picture in some ways equal to a multi-volumed world history.

In another conjunction of the simple and the complex, this area was the geographical setting for the medical research which led to a recent Nobel Prize. The newspaper headline "Both

THE MAN-EATING MYTH

Laureates Found Major Clues in Studies of Primitive Tribesmen"
succinctly brings together the height of western science and its
opposite (Sullivan 1976). Apparently the prevailing opinion of
both modern medical and social science is that the fatal neuro-
logical disorder known in the local language as *kuru* is contracted by eating the insufficiently cooked flesh of human carriers
who also died as the result of their illness. Although the anthropological and medical researchers give different explanations for
the behavior, both agree that cannibalism is a fact of life. The
material on New Guinea cannibalism in general will set the stage
for a specific focus on the Fore and related peoples of the highland area who are the subjects of the extensive *kuru* literature.

The initial stage is reminiscent of the journey through the
African material, since there is a host of references. The major
difference is that in this instance, rather than the bygone traveler,
it is the professional anthropologist of our own era who gives life
to the cannibalism notion. It is scarcely possible to pick up a book
on New Guinea without finding a series of references to cannibalism in the index. Skipping to the actual text results in the
now-familiar vague allusions as each author pays his or her
mandatory respects to the idea.

Margaret Mead was one of the first professional anthropologists to do fieldwork in New Guinea as part of her research in the
Pacific during the 1920s and 1930s. In this age of institutionalized
scholarship, it is easy to fail to appreciate what an extraordinary
personal feat this was and to underestimate the contributions of
this project during the formative years of American anthropology.
In her study of cultural and personality patterns among three
groups in New Guinea, the second chapter, on the Mundugumor,
is called "The Pace of Life in a Cannibal Tribe" (Mead 1950).
The small print in the footnote informs the reader that the former
practice of cannibalism was outlawed by the Australian authorities three years before Mead's arrival. Consequently she did not
directly encounter this or some of the other practices described,
and advises the reader that the present tense is used to refer to the

period three years before her arrival (164). Thus when she says the Mundugumor are cannibals, what she really means is that they were cannibals in the sense of having such a reputation, but she never witnessed the act. In fact, she learned of the Mundugumor passion for human flesh from their neighbors, the "gentle Arapesh."

In addition to setting the literary pattern, Mead is also the first of a long line of anthropologists to display the ability to live among people-eaters in New Guinea without loss of life or limb. A more recent sojourner in the area must be considered even more fortunate, for the "cannibalistic" Jalé, among whom he lived for some time, were reported to have eaten "two white missionaries" in a remote valley of the highlands two years after his departure (Koch 1970a: 41; cf. also Koch 1970b and 1974). The author learned of the anthropophagic bent of the natives prior to his arrival from the published works of missionaries. Although he provides a detailed description of how the Jalé prepared and ate their slain enemies, this was related to him by informants, since the custom was no longer in evidence. The author does not comment directly on this, but it can be assumed that the practice, except for the one regrettable lapse, had been suppressed some years earlier by the authorities (Koch 1974).

The list of New Guinea cannibals and the recorders of their unseen deed is almost endless. Deserving mention at least from among the many candidates are the Asmat, among whom Michael Rockefeller was last seen (Zegwaard 1968), and the Kulai, the object of some of the most recent published fieldwork among reported cannibals. The author writes that most adult members of this tribe have seen a human limb in the smoking rack over the fireplace, and parenthetically adds: "(if they haven't eaten human flesh themselves)" (Schieffelin 1976: 121). As usual, the temptation to spice up the material has proved overwhelming. Finally, there is another recent anthropological report which unabashedly states that the people were so ashamed of cannibalism that they hid it out of a respect for European missionary sensibilities. The text also provides a government patrol officer's comments on these cannibals: "They deny that they eat human flesh, though this interpreter told me not to believe this" (Hallpike 1977: 209-10).

As we close in on the *kuru* area of the highlands, academic standards seem to function as an almost-forgotten ideal, rather than as standard operating procedure. Anthropologists with well-deserved reputations based upon previous research and publication become the victims of their own sensationalism or poor scholarship. The convergence in this instance of both medical and anthropological hypotheses on the existence of cannibalism prepares the way for astounding leaps of fantasy and the demand for the reader to follow along. Berndt's (1962) *Excess and Restraint*, on the *kuru*-stricken Fore, is a case in point, and aptly titled only in the sense that on intellectual grounds it displays too much of the former and too little of the latter. In the author's reference to "excesses," Fore cannibalism figures heavily, even though he mentions that the custom was suppressed just before his appearance in 1951. The lengthy, titillating descriptions of often-combined cannibalistic and sexual acts suggest that prior to his arrival there was nothing that was beyond Fore imagination or practice. Indeed, if there was such a thing as cannibalistic perversion to accompany the sexual variety, the word "Fore" would become synonomous with the idea. However, the suspension of a healthy intellectual skepticism would be called for before one could accept the informants' statements, as presented by Berndt, as literal descriptions of actual occurrences.

For example, the reader is asked to accept an event involving a husband copulating with a female corpse while his wife simultaneously butchers the body for the roasting fire. Unfortunately for him, he is still occupied when his wife's knife draws near, so that she cuts off his penis. Understandably disturbed, but displaying extraordinary equanimity, he asks, "now you have cut off my penis! What shall I do?" In response, his wife "popped it into her mouth, and ate it . . . ." (283).

This is a harsh punishment for adultery, but could Fore behavior, not to mention physiology, be so far removed from what we and the rest of the world accept as conforming to common standards? A double dose of cannibalism with sadism and necrophilia all at once makes it difficult to determine which of the reader's sensibilities has suffered the most. However, a moment's reflection suggests that common sense has been the primary object of this assault. Scholarship meanwhile has become an irrelevant consideration, as sensationalism becomes the ideal. Those who would claim that we have to take the author's word that this actually took place should consider the work of the following more objective students of the ethnographic material.

Berndt also refers the reader to examples of similar cannibalistic "behavior" contained in Landtman's study *The Folk Tales of the Kiwai Papuans* (1917). In addition to the Kiwai's being hundreds of miles away from the Fore, Landtman makes it explicit in his introduction that his material consists of folk tales, not descriptions of events. Therefore, in no way does his data confirm Berndt's material. His excellent ethnography (Landtman 1927) of Kiwai culture published some years later, based on two years of fieldwork, makes no mention of cannibalism among the Kiwai. Rather, his detailed discussion of death indicates elaborate ceremonials and deference paid to the deceased, who is interred in full dress and ornamentation amid great mourning. Indeed, instead of eating him, a wife dutifully attends to her husband's gravesite for an extended period. Further, as an indication of the fear of the pollution associated with the dead, the bed and burial platform of the deceased are burned. Finally, those who have come into contact with the corpse must ritually purify themselves before resuming normal social intercourse (254–66). However, the author does point out that one Kiwai informant told him of a neighboring people who not only cook and eat their own dead, but sometimes hasten their demise lest the body fat diminish before it can be put to use for the benefit of the living. The informant added that this was done in secret, and any stranger to put in an appearance at these gruesome occasions would be killed (267). It might be best to conclude with the charitable notion that naiveté prevented another ethnographer from realizing that these neighboring people are in truth the habitués of Kiwai folk tales.

A more extensive analysis of Berndt's monograph on the Fore would serve no useful purpose. The book has already indicated some of the potential limits of contemporary anthropology in New Guinea. Subsequent research by others helps to restore a sense of confidence, and permits a more positive consideration of the problem. This is also the best moment to begin to meld the ethnographic and medical evidence for cannibalism by considering in more detail the disease of *kuru*. I undertake this charge with the sense of modesty instilled by the existence of a two-hundred-page bibliography on the topic, with over fifteen hundred citations to the scientific and ethnographic literature (Alpers et al. 1975). The task is made manageable by the fact that my only concern here is the role the consumption of human flesh is suspected of playing in the transmission of the illness.

The entire literature is beyond the scope and mastery of any single individual. The procedure I adopted was first to gain a general grasp of the medical material through a careful reading of the most up-to-date and instructive synopses. Second, I reviewed some of the earliest publications in order to determine how the idea came to make its significant appearance that cannibalism was the suspected agent of transmission of the disease. Third, I considered the entire relevant ethnographic record in light of the related medical assumptions. Some general ethnographic and medical background permits a better understanding of the more detailed subsequent items.

The east-central highland area in question was not entered by Europeans until 1932, when the now-familiar adventurers, this time in the form of gold prospectors and Protestant missionaries, made their appearance. But the outbreak of the second World War prevented anything more than sporadic contact with the resident groups until 1950.

Despite linguistic differences, for present purposes the highland area can be seen as sharing common social, cultural and ecologic patterns. These include a varying reliance on the sweet potato, a "pig complex" most apparent on ceremonial occasions, "big men" rather than appointed office-holders and inter-village warfare involving an alliance system. At the local level, communities normally contained at most a few hundred individuals claiming some sort of kinship tie to everyone else based upon descent or marriage. Traditionally, the villages were surrounded by a stockade fence, and adult men and young boys lived in a men's house, while a married woman with her younger male children and daughters resided in a single dwelling. Prior to contact, the women and children were responsible for cultivation and care of the pigs, while the men dabbled in the political and military arts. Finally, among the Fore and neighboring linguistic groups who suffered from *kuru*, the women were also supposed to be the cannibals.

The word *kuru* itself means "trembling," since this is the first and most obvious symptom of the illness, which the Fore assume is caused by sorcery. According to their belief, a sorcerer uses some bodily substance or personal item of another which, when placed in a small bundle with magical substances and regularly shaken, causes the victim to contract and eventually die of *kuru*. The only cure is to identify the culprit and force him or her to cease these activities. It is rarely successful, since in almost every instance death occurs. Western science prefers to believe that the misfortune belongs to the recently identified "slow-virus" category of disease, is not precisely sure how it is contracted, and has no cure, so that death is a foregone conclusion. Thus, on the vital issue of life and death, the difference between the savage and the civilized is not profound.

Like those of many other scientific discoveries, the story of *kuru* unravels like a first-rate mystery novel. In addition to the crime, there is an obvious culprit lurking somewhere, a host of clues, false leads, disappointing setbacks and of course the detective and his cronies. The story also contains the loose ends which so often unsettle the *aficionado* of this literary genre. But these can only be savored after having gone through the entire plot. In this case, it begins with the appearance of D. Carleton Gajdusek, M.D., the central character of the piece and as colorful as any novelist's sleuth.

The future Nobel laureate arrived in New Guinea in 1957 with no purpose except a sense of adventure and curiosity after a two-year stint in Australia as a visiting fellow at a research institute. While visiting the highlands he met by chance Vincent Zigas, a local medical officer, who introduced Gajdusek to the Fore and *kuru*. Although he was on his way back to America, Gajdusek became intrigued enough to stay among the Fore for ten months, investigating this rare and strange disease. He and his associates eventually published a score of articles, and Gajdusek has made available his letters from the field to his nominal superior in the Washington federal medical bureaucracy (Gajdusek 1976). As a whole this material allows the outsider an unprecedented opportunity to follow the scientific and personal drama.

Kuru was first mentioned in the routine reports of Australian colonial patrol officers who administered the area until independence. Berndt was the first to describe the symptoms, which in addition to tremors involve euphoria, in a series of articles which introduced the Fore to the anthropological world. In this otherwise informative series, he defined *kuru* as a psychosomatic disorder brought on by the shock of contact with the European world (Berndt 1952 and 1954). Zigas, however, was aware that almost a hundred percent of those afflicted died within twelve months of the onset of the symptoms, so that his argument had greater influence on Gajdusek. Zigas had previously tried to interest the colonial and Australian medical hierarchy in this phenomenon, but to no avail. In contrast, Gajdusek immediately realized the potential significance of the situation and seized the opportunity. He wrote to Washington at once, informing his contact that he was taking up residence in the highlands of New Guinea among "tribal groups of cannibals" who would even eat the body of someone who had died of the very disease he had decided to study (Gajdusek 1976: 50). As an indication of his commitment, he added that he had no money for this unanticipated research or personal funds, except for some savings which he would begin to draw on. He asked for and later received, as a financial sign of the times, one thousand dollars to support his activities, with the unsolicited advice from the administrative officer that it was about time he settled down and learned to take care of himself. The author of this sage counsel and recipient of many of Gajdusek's letters was a well-intentioned friend ensconced in the Washington bureaucracy. Not surprisingly, he figured little in subsequent scientific advances. With such meager funds and encouragement, Gajdusek and Zigas set out to systematically investigate this problem.

The research was neither simple nor easy. Epidemiological concerns necessitated arduous foot patrols into uncharted areas in order to plot the distribution and incidence of the illness, while treatment of the patients and allied research were conducted in a hospital hastily put together from local materials. The two principals soon confirmed their suspicion that they were dealing with a mysterious disease rather than a peculiar expression of culture shock. They also learned that the *kuru* area, of approximately 250 square miles, encompassed only the Fore territory and segments of some adjacent highland groups, but among them the disease was raging at epidemic proportions. Within a few months, Gajdusek and Zigas were able to isolate two hundred cases in an area containing twenty thousand people, indicating that one percent of the population was affected, which meant that *kuru* was responsible for one half of all deaths that year. The epidemiology of the malady was the trifling aspect of the problem, in contrast to the matters of origin and transmission.

The restriction of the disease to this one area of the highlands immediately suggested the probability of an inherited genetic

THE MAN-EATING MYTH

factor resulting in a degeneration of the central nervous system. If the symptoms had appeared randomly in relation to age and sex, the case would have been a simple one, but there was a troublesome problem with this genetic hypothesis. At the time, there were fifteen cases of *kuru* among females for every one among males, while for children it never appeared prior to four and a half years, but the sex ratio of the victims was equal. There were also four adult cases of the disease for every one among children. Simply put, *kuru* appeared to be primarily a disease affecting adult women and to a lesser extent children of both sexes. (Gajdusek 1968: 165 and 1976: 142). The fact that adult men also succumbed, but only rarely, implied that the genetic hypothesis by itself failed to explain the problem adequately. There might be a genetic predisposition, but only operating in conjunction with other unknown factors which would have to be accounted for by other means.

There was one further problem with the genetic hypothesis which related to the history of the disease, as provided by Fore informants. The medical team considered this line of investigation in some detail, but then dismissed the problem as stemming from unreliable data (Gajdusek and Zigas 1961). The Fore, who Gajdusek admits provided remarkably consistent information on the incidence of the disease, said that *kuru* claimed its first victims at the beginning of this century. Gajdusek and Zigas concluded that this sort of chronological reckoning was beyond a cultural group without a calendar or written records. However, this opinion was not shared by anthropologists with experience among the Fore, who were later to be instrumental in proposing an explanation for the disease's imbalanced sex ratio.

While in the field, Gajdusek and Zigas sought environmental clues which they felt might be responsible for triggering the disease. As interest in their project spread, they were joined by a nutritionist who subjected the Fore diet to an intensive analysis in the search for toxic agents or some other type of nutritional peculiarity. Botanists and entomologists made research forays to investigate local flora and insects which were part of the normal diet. These leads proved unprofitable, but speculation continued. The fact that women and children spent more time in smoke-filled huts seemed promising until laboratory tests of the ashes failed to uncover any toxic elements. Meanwhile, the two researchers tried to examine every *kuru* patient and ironically bartered for the corpses of *kuru* victims. These were submitted to crude autopsies in the field, while bodily fluids and vital organs, especially brain sections, were sent off to America for more sophisticated analysis. Although this resulted in further information on the character and symptoms of the disease, they learned nothing about the cause of the illness. Gajdusek provides no direct information on what the natives made of all this, but does mention in passing that over the months they turned from cooperative into recalcitrant research subjects (1976). An objective observer from another planet, with no prior knowledge of the customs of either the Fore or the Westerners, would have little difficulty in concluding which group had the inexplicable interest in human remains.

However, this was not to be, for in time the cannibal label was securely pinned on the Fore. The process by which this took place, however, was also vague and ambiguous. A careful reading of the numerous published reports by the principals does not always provide a clear-cut version of the events. Starting the reconstruction with a foreknowledge gained from the most recent statements, with their fixation on cannibalism, and working backwards produces some unexpected results. This path is worth following, for when I began to consider the general problem of cannibalism I was informed that I need not go further, since a scientist had proved that a rare disease in New Guinea was transmitted by cannibalism. The subsequent awarding of the Nobel Prize for this research should have been enough to convince anyone of the scientific validity of the cannibalism notion, but it does not turn out this way.

Gajdusek's (1976) correspondence from the field in 1957,

referred to before, provides the best point of access to the flow of ideas. As indicated, his first letter defined the Fore as cannibals, and it is probably best to assume that this was impressed on him by common enough hearsay, since he was there for only a few days before penning the words. It can also be safely assumed that he saw no actual evidence of the act in the ten months, or he would have mentioned the fact in print, though he refers on two occasions to information on anthropophagic reports. In one instance, he writes that one of his native friends reported that a relative had eaten their common grandfather. However, Gajdusek adds that it is unlikely that all *kuru* patients could have eaten infected human brains or ectoderm. He concludes: "It is so unique a concept, and such a romantic one, that I almost wish cannibalism was more prevalent than it is" (234). He reconsidered the idea later, and again ruled it out (300). In spite of these disclaimers, the significance of cannibalism figures in letters he receives from colleagues in America, urging him to consider something in the Fore diet or an item possibly eaten at a ceremony (191, 253). His more cautious governmental colleague, referred to earlier, also began to worry that some indigene might "revert to cannibalism" and eat Gajdusek's brain, which was chock-full of vital unrecorded scientific data. He advised Gajdusek to finish up his work and "get the hell back here" (177).

Still undeterred by such sane counsel, Gajdusek remained, in the hopes of hitting upon the cause and means of transmission of *kuru*. He and Zigas also began to submit their preliminary findings to medical journals, and it is worth noting in passing that the first piece announcing the discovery of this disease was rejected by the editor of a prominent and widely read scientific magazine. The item which appeared in the same publication some twenty years later heralding Gajdusek's genius and Nobel Prize, naturally enough failed to mention this small fact (Marsh 1976). Incredibly enough, their report barely passed the editorial board of a respected but regional medical journal, where it did see the light of day shortly thereafter. In all the earliest publications, the Fore are characterized as "New Guinea cannibals," but there is no suggestion at the time that this is related in any way to the disease (Gajdusek and Zigas 1957; Zigas and Gajdusek 1957; Zigas and Gajdusek 1959; Gajdusek and Zigas 1961; Gajdusek 1963; and Alpers 1966). In fact, in 1965 Gajdusek wrote that he had considered a possible relationship between the illness and cannibalism but soon dismissed this unlikely idea, because there was no evidence that *kuru* patients even participated in such an act (Gajdusek 1965). Some time earlier, he had reported that the "outlandish hypothesis" of cannibalism as a transmission agent was not substantiated by laboratory tests (Gajdusek 1963: 162). However, by 1970, Gajdusek and others now associated with the study of *kuru* were discussing cannibalism during rituals as "a strange mode of transmission" (Gajdusek 1970: 128), calling it "a reasonable hypothesis" (Gibbs and Gajdusek 1974: 45), and saying that its suppression provided a means to explain the decline of the disease (Alpers 1970: 136). The abrupt about-face on this issue occurred for various reasons.

Until 1965, Gajdusek and his associates were tentatively committed to the idea of a genetic predisposition activated by an environmental agent to account for the onset of *kuru*. Consequently, the cannibalism notion was neither a necessary nor a particularly attractive hypothesis. However, this orientation was attacked on a number of fronts by various specialists. Generally they were of the opinion that what was known about the disease, especially age and sex ratios, did not accord with existing medical and scientific knowledge in the field of genetics (Hornabrook 1975: 84–85).

Simultaneously anthropologists, who were more apt to consider the relationship between cultural and medical phenomena, further undermined the genetic position and began to draw tentative connections between the possibility of Fore cannibalism and *kuru* (Fischer and Fischer 1960, 1961 and 1962). Although it was yet to be identified, there was some suspicion even at this time that *kuru* could be a virus and thus infectious through close

THE MAN-EATING MYTH

contact in any number of ways. With the increasing notoriety and potential scientific significance of the disease, two other social anthropologists took up residence among the Fore, previously studied by Berndt, to investigate the social and cultural effects of *kuru* on the population. In a series of reports, the senior member of the team began to introduce more forcefully the idea of cannibalism as the transmission agent of *kuru* (Glasse 1962, 1963, 1967 and 1970). Meanwhile, Gajdusek had returned to America, and in collaboration with others was able to transmit the disease in the laboratory from infected human brain tissue of a *kuru* victim to chimpanzees, demonstrating that the disease was caused by an active virus rather than a genetic weakness (Gajdusek et al. 1966). The anthropological fixation on cannibalism in the field therefore became more compatible with laboratory experiments.

The question, as always, is: What evidence is there to support the now-prevailing notion that cannibalism, as opposed to some other form of close contact, is the principal means of transmitting the fatal infection among the Fore (Glasse and Lindenbaum 1976 and Gajdusek 1977a)? As usual, the evidence is circumstantial, since Fore cannibalism has never been observed by an outsider. As indicated, Berndt (1962) pointed out that the custom had been suppressed three years before his arrival in the early 1950s, while Glasse writes that it was abolished four years before his arrival in the late 1950s (1967). Rather than assuming, as the previous information allows, that cannibalism has a sporadic revival whenever there are no anthropologists to observe it, we can conclude instead that if it ever existed, cannibalism was no longer extant when the ethnographers were present. As a result, Glasse and Lindenbaum relied upon Berndt's idiosyncratic discussion of the material, the fact that the Fore had a reputation among surrounding groups for eating their dead, the odd report that someone had eaten someone else and the belief among the males that "the great majority of women" were cannibals (Glasse 1967: 751). There are other factors which, when added to the assumption of cannibalism, result in a fairly strong and consistent case for this particular transmission hypothesis. First, Glasse (1962) argues that the Fore became cannibals at the turn of the century, which conforms to their statements about the initial appearance of the disease. Second, the Fore idea of the proclivity of only women to eat human flesh would account for the age-sex distribution of the disease, since a mother would be likely to pass on infected tissue of a human victim to young children of both sexes. Third, there has been a gradual decline in *kuru* deaths since the height of the disease in 1961, just after the appearance an effective European presence which would have stamped out any remaining vestiges of cannibalism. Taken together, these factors produce a clear-cut association between two phenomena. However, there is room for caution. First, by anyone's standards, this is an association only, not a demonstrated cause-and-effect relationship. Second, the association is between the disappearance of an act which was never observed and what is in some ways a still-mysterious disease.

There are further problems with the hypothesis that *kuru* is transmitted by eating insufficiently cooked human flesh. Rather than uncritically accepting the native view that only women and children are cannibals, it would seem reasonable to question whether or not this might be a symbolic statement about females, in a culture area renowned for sexual antagonism and opposition and among a specific people who have raised the process to a cultural art (Lindenbaum 1976). Further, although in one place Glasse (1967) provides a detailed description of how the Fore butcher prepares dead bodies, in a later co-authored publication (Glasse and Lindenbaum 1976), we learn that specialists are called upon to prepare the deceased for burial, since contact with a corpse is thought to be dangerous. The contradictions implied deserve recognition and evaluation. How a human body could be viewed as something to be both eaten and avoided is a conundrum, unless possibly the males assume that it is in the nature of females to break the most basic taboos. This attitude would be consistent, though, in a society with a system of symbolic oppositions in which women, "like the red pandanus trees, are only partly tamed" (Lindenbaum 1976: 56). Since they are not completely human, they are liable to revert to a state of nature.

An earlier publication by Berndt (1958) and another some time later by Glasse (1970) support the contention that some of the cultural material should be submitted to a symbolic analysis, rather than accepted at face value as fact. As mentioned, according to the Fore view *kuru* is the result of a brand of sorcery, and discussion with informants on two typical cases shows a "stylized formula" of a Fore woman who, having married into a neighboring hostile group, is killed by sorcery in her husband's community and "then eaten by her murderers" (Berndt 1958: 12–13). Too many similar supernatural visions of the relationship between evil-doers and cannibalism prevail in other parts of New Guinea and the world to allow us to admit this as evidence for an actual human activity. Another anthropologist reports that among a neighboring group, one-half of the sizable number of homicides involve a woman victim who has been suspected of killing and eating another by supernatural means. He points out that the nature of the crime itself does not permit a consideration of actual evidence, since none exists (Steadman 1975).

Another reasonable suspicion of the cannibalism hypothesis is aroused by the fact that among the Fore each death is followed by a mortuary feast involving the slaughter of pigs and distribution of the meat and vegetables (Glasse and Lindenbaum, 1976). This period of an abundance of animal protein would seem to be the least likely time to resort to cannibalism. Finally, if fear of ritual pollution and availability of a sanctioned meat source were insufficient causes for caution regarding the belief in the transmission of *kuru* by ingestion, the realization that it is most closely related in man to Creutzfeld-Jakob's disease demands a more comparative perspective. Although rare, this second unconventional viral infection has a worldwide distribution, which raises the obvious question of how the illness is communicated elsewhere. Having discussed cannibalism as a "reasonable" way to account for the *kuru* problem, Gibbs and Gajdusek (1974) conclude that no such hypothesis exists to explain the transmission of Creutzfeld-Jakob's disease. No one has yet suggested that this and other suspected puzzling slow-virus maladies, which include Parkinson's disease, multiple sclerosis, and certain types of measles (Gajdusek 1977), are transmitted in the western world by cannibalism. However, such a hypothesis presents no problem when the affected population is the inhabitants of the New Guinea highlands. This is consistent with the general theoretical tone of much of the anthropological literature on this area, which effectively diminishes the cultural achievements of the inhabitants. For example, a well-known study of a religious system in the area (Rappaport 1968) is primarily a treatment of the relationship between ecology, nutrition and ritual. The subjective meaning and content of the religion, which are primarily products of the human mind rather than the environment, receive comparatively little attention. When ecological perimeters take precedence over cultural concerns in anthropological studies, then the notion of cannibalism as an adaptive response to protein deficiency becomes a consistent and reasonable view of human nature in this part of the world as it has been for others.

As suggested at the outset of this discussion, there are a number of loose ends still in sight if one is prepared to proceed with an open mind. The existence of scientific hypothesis should not prevent others from reflecting on the problem, especially if the present position depends upon a blending of speculative information from various disciplines. Again, in this case, it is impossible to prove that cannibalism is not a factor in the *kuru* syndrome. However, I have sought to show that, rather than a firm scientific position on cannibalism, the situation actually involves a hypothesis based upon circumstantial evidence. Further, there are certain contradictions in the ethnography, while the same material lends itself to alternate interpretations.

Suggesting some alternate explanations for *kuru*, based upon a modicum of common knowledge, permits a more positive conclusion. Surprisingly enough, no one has seriously considered the idea that the presence of Europeans in the area was responsible for the outbreak of the epidemic at the turn of the century. The arrival of the first two Europeans in 1932 does not deny the possible entry of the disease years before through indirect means and intermediaries. In point of fact, the statistics on the disease show an increase, as contact with outsiders increases, until the peak in 1961, and then a gradual decline (Glasse 1962). The decrease in mortality also coincides with radical change in all aspects of native life, ranging from hygienic practices to domestic arrangements, as the Fore were overrun with European technology and emissaries. This means that there are numerous associations between changes in Fore customs and the mortality trends. In light of the obvious cultural rearrangements and new experiences, it is odd that scientific researchers have seized on a correlation between something which was never seen and another phenomenon studied and measured so meticulously.

One of the most profound alterations in Fore social patterns resulting from European contact involved new household arrangements; the husband-father moved into the same dwelling with his wife and children, since the men's house fell into disuse. The traditional and new domestic arrangements were significant in relation to *kuru* for a number of reasons. First, the mother-offspring living pattern would provide the ideal setting for easy transmission of a virus between women and children, since they were in close contact. The males, on the other hand, although not isolated, were less likely to come into contact or remain with *kuru* victims. Young males who moved into the men's house would have already demonstrated their resistance to the virus and thus not infect their colleagues. The second point of potential importance relates to the increase in the number of males to come down with the illness as these new domestic patterns emerged. The movement of men into the nuclear-family household also coincided with an increased male mortality rate caused by *kuru* (Hornabrook and Moir 1970). Proposing an increase in hidden male cannibalism to account for this relationship would be too absurd when more obvious clues abound.

The argument proposed here contains nothing original, since the manifestation of diseases in epidemic proportions is a common accompaniment of human-contact situations. From this vantage point, it is impossible to demonstrate the validity of the thesis; but it is reasonable rather than "outlandish"—which is how Gajdusek once described the cannibalism notion. What is most surprising is the failure of those more closely related to the problem to consider this approach in print. Gajdusek (1976) did give the idea some thought while in the earliest stage of his stay in New Guinea, but at the time he was unaware that he was dealing with a transmittable virus. The genetic predisposition idea resulted in his dismissal of the theory. However, it seems worth reconsidering at this time, along with alternative explanations which do not require cannibalism as a factor. In the words of another scientist interested in this problem: "It would be unfortunate if too easy acceptance of the cannibalism hypothesis should handicap further inquiry into the pathogenesis of *kuru*" (Burnet 1971: 5).

However, maintaining an open mind is no simple matter once the experts close in on a suspected, even though unproved, hypothesis. This is demonstrated by an examination of Gajdusek's (1977b) most recent summary of the present thinking on unconventional slow viruses and *kuru* in particular, which vividly conveys the imagery of Fore cannibalism as the transmission agent. This article by the Nobel laureate contains two compelling photographs (Gajdusek 1977: 956). The first is a picture of a Fore woman who has just died of *kuru*, while the second, just below, shows a group of Fore sitting around an earth oven, feasting on an obscure but obviously tasty meal. The accompanying text mentions how the Fore prepared the endocannibalistic meals in such ovens and how infection was most probably the result of butchery and the handling of cooked meat. Anyone who did not conclude he was now staring solid documentation in the face would deserve a reward for recalcitrance. However, such a distinction is undeserved, since subsequent inquiries revealed that this was not an actual photographic sequence of cannibalism, but rather an attempt by the author, in the absence of available visual evidence, to illustrate what he believes to be a common parallel practice among the Fore. Thus the photograph showing the Fore in the midst of a meal actually involves the consumption of a pig, not the *kuru* victim shown in the previous scene (Gajdusek 1978).

During the course of the investigation of this topic, a series of personal communications with Gajdusek (1978) which he was kind enough to respond to, although helpful, did not completely resolve this matter. However, while this book was in press, Gajdusek began to treat the cannibal notion more cautiously, since he is now quoted as saying that "there has been so far no convincing evidence that the infection can be acquired by eating or drinking affected material or by any means other than direct invasion of the bloodstream" (Schmeck 1978: 16).

This chapter has demonstrated that the two most popularly assumed instances of institutionalized cannibalism of our era also lack the first-hand documentation which characterized the Carib and Aztec cases. As usual, the absence of hard and fast evidence in these latter-day examples is explained in terms of the recent cessation of the traditional practice. A more specific contrast between the two eras and their most prominent anthropophagic areas reaveals further ideological parallels of note. The Caribbean and Africa functioned as free-floating cannibal arenas, with little documentation expected or forthcoming. The amusing racial slur seemed to be sufficient evidence. By contrast, for reasons peculiar to each era, the Aztecs as a specific complex social system and the Fore as representatives of the last preserve of savagery on the present fringe of western civilization were converted into cannibals by the most prominent and respected ideological systems available at the time. The Aztec case in the sixteenth century was supported by the weight of explicit religious morality and scholarship in conjunction with the contributions of the first ethnographers. The Fore instance of the twentieth century is shored up by the medical sciences and the now-institutionalized discipline of social anthropology. The handmaiden role of the interpreters of human custom is not fortuitous. Before turning to this problem in detail, two intervening steps are called for.

The problem requires, however briefly, a consideration of the evidence on the possibility of cannibalism derived from physical anthropology and archeology. This is not an unrelated matter, since the views of our own dim past and of distant foreign cultures assumed to have been mired in this pristine state often reinforce each other.

IV

THE PREHISTORIC WORLD OF ANTHROPOPHAGY

Having traversed the historic record for the past five hundred years in search of the cannibal and finding the record obscured by the passage of time, it may seem out of temporal sequence, if not futile, to approach now the fossilized evidence for this phenomenon. However, this is called for, since the ever-compelling possibility of man eating man at the dawn of human history is never far from the thoughts of paleontologists, physical anthropologists, archeologists and prehistorians. Furthermore, the task is manageable, for when people in these disciplines stray from their realms of expertise, begin to muse on the primal nature of the beast and attempt to drape the bones and stones with a cultural mantle, they have little choice but to draw on the work of their colleagues in social anthropology who study more contemporary primitive man. This means that, although the actual physcial material may be as old as the species itself, the conclusions are reflections of the contemporary era.

Cannibals abound as western science pushes back the frontiers of time. There are at least two reasons for this. First, all the academic branches which today are classed under the heading of modern anthropology emerged as organized inquiries at the same time, facing one overriding question. The formative period extended from the mid-nineteenth to the turn of the twentieth century, and the intellectual puzzle, which remains unsolved and is still debated, was the original human condition. The industrializing western societies were bringing the remainder of the globe under European colonial domination in an almost effortless, unchecked process of expansion. At this apex of their power, intellectuals in an institutionalized setting and systematic fashion first began to ponder the historical path to this assumed inevitable conclusion. They had no doubts but that they were the end product of an evolutionary sequence, and from the written historical record were fairly knowledgeable about some of the more recent prior stages. However, they were far less certain and eminently more cautious about the primeval past, which was still beclouded by biblical interpretations of creation and human progress or the lack of such. A break with this sacred paradigm was clearly required if advances were to be made in the form of a rational, secular study of mankind. The first language, the most primitive social institutions and original man himself would have to be reconstructed by recovering the physical and cultural artifacts in conjunction with more detailed information on non-western societies, which were thought to have remained in early evolutionary phases. In this fashion, an equation was made between nineteenth-century primitives and prehistoric man. Both creatures were assumed to be almost devoid of culture as conceived by the European mind of the last century; and in this savage state, the worst could be expected.

This line of reasoning inevitably led to the second reason for the *a priori* assumption of cannibalism on the part of early man. The forerunners of modern anthropology were already steeped in information from travelers and missionaries on the cannibalistic bent of their exotic contemporaries who were still to encounter the full weight of western civilization. (This burden would of course entail refusing to allow them to indulge their taste for human flesh.) Consequently, if nineteenth-century primitives living close to the state of nature were known to be prone to cannibalism, then should not the same hold for the original primitives from whom we are all descended? The nineteenth-century imagination viewed European civilization as an imperiled bastion hemmed in by both temporal and spatial borders across which were ogres.

This self-fulfilling prophecy was not long in providing the documentary evidence from the earth which was to give horrible credence to the worst fears. One archeologist interested in the fact or fiction of prehistoric cannibalism mentions that in 1865, during the very first years of this discipline as a profession, cannibalism was associated with one of the earliest recorded finds. He quotes the report of the proto-archeologist, who wrote: "It appears to me, that, in these broken skulls and disjointed bones we have the result of feasts" (in Brothwell 1961: 304). This tentative assertion, based primarily on the mere fact that the human skeletal remains were not in perfect condition, received some early support, but was soon rejected for two compelling reasons. First, the remains were found in the Yorkshire region of Britain itself, and second, they were dated to the all-too-recent Iron Age of a scant two thousand years earlier, which immediately preceded the Roman era. In this instance, the boundaries of the savage mode of existence were drawn too close for comfort. However, the same strictures were not to hold for the more ancient remains of early man which began to emerge in the non-western world. Similar precautions would no longer be necessary in the subsequent ruminations on the possible significance of the less-than-perfect human remains. In these instances the imagination of prehistorians could express itself more freely and grandly, which it soon did, and often continues to do.

When the calendar is pushed back to the Pleistocene, of three million to ten thousand years ago, the cannibal theme begins to flourish in a more hospitable temporal climate. The list of cannibals and victims of the nefarious deed reads like a *Who's Who* of physical anthropology, and includes *Australopithecus, Homo erectus, Homo neanderthalensis,* and of course *Homo sapiens* himself. These inclusive categories pinpoint cannibalism for all of the Old World and subsume some of the more familiar names from the past, such as Java Man, Pekin Man, and Cro-Magnon Man. The list is so extensive because, as one archeologist put it, without considering alternatives cannibalism is "the favored explanation" for human remains, which are invariably broken (Brothwell 1961: 304). Again we encounter an odd state of affairs for a presumedly scientific discipline which demands more rigorous methods when other problems are being scrutinized.

To be fair, some standards are maintained, so there is debate in the professional literature, but these skeptical forays are rare, and fail to find their way into the more popular archeological magazines. The typical modern textbook usually gleefully points out either that prehistoric homonoids were eaters of their own kind or that there is strong evidence to suggest this was the case. Alternate explanations of a less fantastic nature to account for the condition of the fossils are rarely considered, since this would make for less stimulating discussion. The popular literature on human nature which is presently enjoying such a boom makes no pretense to scientific objectivity. Although often well-written by erudite and clever popularizers, these contributions draw attention to the difference between knowledge and comprehension. Thus Ardrey, one of the most vocal figures of this school, can glibly write, "Cannibalism has been a prevalent pastime throughout all of the human record" (1976: 263). It is not easy to combat such vagaries, but fortunately he later becomes more specific. Discussing one of the favorite assumed cannibals from man's past, he writes: "I do not know of a competent authority who disagrees with the great student of Pekin Man, Franz Weidenreich, that they were head-hunters and cannibals" (163–64). As we shall see shortly, many of the most respected figures of paleontology fail to succumb as easily to preconceived ideologies about the nature of man and allied prehistoric species. Surprisingly enough, this includes that "great student of Pekin Man," Franz Weidenreich himself, who is more cautious than the enthusiastic Ardrey. In his final and most extensive consideration of Pekin Man, or *Sinanthropus*, Weidenreich (1943) mentions that although he had tentatively considered the cannibal hypothesis in earlier essays, he is able to provide other reasonable explanations for the damaged condition of the fossils. In the process, he demonstrates that more than scientific jargon distinguishes scholarship from vulgarity.

Pekin Man has already crept into the discussion, and the controversy about his base nature provides a typical, illuminating example of some contemporary thinking about the primitive past. The fossilized objects in question were found in a limestone cave near Choukoutien, China, about thirty miles from Peking, in a series of excavations carried out by European paleontologists between 1926 and 1941. From these fossilized Sinanthropoid remains of at least forty individuals in the form of scattered and fragmented crania, mandibles, teeth and splintered limb bones, the researchers were able to piece together fifteen more or less complete adult skulls dating to approximately a half million years ago. The fact that most of the bones were damaged crania also showing signs of an artificially enlarged opening at the base around the *foramen magnum* immediately suggested to some of the more fertile minds that these unfortunates were the victims of foul play. Moreover, the broken base hinted to others of a similar bent that this was done so that the brains could be eaten by the perpetrators, which to the sensationalists "commemorates the ancient practice of man eat man" (Coon 1963: 600). Yet to the more jaundiced eye this is a dubious proposition.

Other potential explanations may lack the dramatic quality of homicide and cannibalism, but they do have common sense and experience on their side. For example, it has been pointed out that the almost complete absence of other skeletal parts in the Choukoutien deposits implies that the human remains were not brought into the cave as food. The more complete distribution pattern of animal remains, which make up a more considerable part of the material found in the caves, indicates these were the primary food supply for Pekin Man (Breuil and Lantier 1965: 232). Indeed, if these cavemen had been dining on each other, the least choice part would have been the head, which is almost devoid of flesh. This presents no insurmountable problem to those who refuse to have their prejudices uprooted. Their response is to propose that the brain as a human delicacy was the object of the anthropophagic quest. The suspicion that this desire was motivated not out of hunger but in the attempt to somehow consume the essence of the deceased in a sacred ritual (Leakey and

Lewin 1977: 132) would impute to these cavemen, who were just beginning to appreciate the quality of fire, the possession of some fairly sophisticated knowledge of human neurology and anatomy. The high frequency of similar human remains in Australopithecine sites of Africa for an earlier period has been laid to the work of carnivorous animals, who may have feasted on this creature but were unable to ingest the jaws, skulls and upper cervical vertebrae (Washburn 1957: 613). This evidence from the Australopithecine sites suggests that the same sequence of events might hold for the Choukoutien site, with Pekin Man having fallen prey before or after death to predators who dragged the remains into unoccupied rock shelters.

The general condition of the bones and skulls is no great mystery, either, since we have it on good authority that the damage can more realistically be explained as the consequence of their having been crushed by falling debris from the ceilings of the caves over the centuries. In fact, fossils from this era for any part of the world are rarely recovered in good condition (Shapiro 1974: 84). Again, to the closed minds, this would mean that everyone was eating everyone they could lay their hands on, which more befits the image of prehistoric and contemporary savagery. Finally, Montagu's review of the evidence makes the telling point that, in addition to the absence of teeth marks, only one of the human fragments showed doubtful signs of having been charred. In contrast, the associated animal bones from the kitchen middens of Pekin Man indicated that they had been cooked (Montagu 1976: 109–10).

The enlarged opening around the base of the skull, which is also a feature of many other prehistoric hominid finds, is another matter. Alternate explanations for this condition will be as speculative as the cannibalism hypothesis, but no less credible. Montagu, who writes on this topic as a practicing anatomist, argues that extracting the brain through an enlarged opening at the base of the skull would be a much more difficult process than simply smashing the bone cover to get at the inner tissue. He proposes therefore that this more careful and laborious method suggests that a primary object was the preservation of the skull in an intact form (1976: 118). The rationale for this procedure would be the intention of the living to keep the skull of the deceased as a reminder of his former presence. This may first appear to the uninitiated as a rather bizarre custom, but the decoration of living quarters with the skull of a departed had a widespread distribution until the present century. Therefore, the possibility that Pekin Man, as well as many other prehistoric groups, might have employed such a funerary device is not as far-fetched as might be imagined.

Possibly the best way to lay the idea of brain-eating to rest is to refer to the work of an eminent paleontologist who set out to weigh the evidence for this prehistoric possibility by comparing it to the accounts of existing cannibals with similar tastes. Assuming, from the allusions of the general publications, that this practice also had a widespread occurrence in recent times, he was apparently shocked to find the documentation unavailable. As someone accustomed to dealing with hard facts, he wrote in a disgruntled fashion, "the author has not succeeded in finding in the literature a first-hand, detailed account describing the actual practice from beginning to end, even without photographs or film documentation" (Jacob 1972: 82). As usual, when attempts are made to go beyond the realm of second- and third-hand news for evidence, the print dries up. Ironically enough, the same holds true for the object of so much present speculation on prehistoric cannibalism, for the fossil remains of Pekin Man disappeared in 1941. Extinct bones, like extinct cultures, always seem to provide the best evidence for cannibalism.

Not all of the more ancient evidence for cannibalism has disappeared. Moving now to the New World, we find that archeologists have uncovered for various times and places an abundance of human remains which suggest some dark doings prior to the arrival of the white man. In general, the material and interpretive conclusions are not as clouded by those who claim insights into the moral philosophy of primitive man. In some instances the reports often lend some direct credence to the idea that the North American aborigines may have experimented with or resorted to cannibalism, but sensational broad generalizations still have to be guarded against.

A typical recent example comes from the American Southwest, dating to the Pueblo period of 900 to 1300 A.D. (Flinn et al. 1976). The human evidence involves the remains of a presumed domestic unit composed of eleven individuals of all ages and sexes who come to their violent end in a single dwelling in northern New Mexico sometime around 950 A.D. The skeletons were fragmented, with some parts missing, the skulls smashed; the long bones were crushed, exposing the marrow cavities, and along with the cranial parts they showed signs of cut marks and of having been charred. These two latter features are not characteristic of other prehistoric burial sites for the same time and place, so the evidence for cannibalism is pointed. Nevertheless the authors carefully weigh other explanations and indicate that some of the features could have been caused by other means than cannibalism. They choose the cannibalism hypothesis because the house itself was not burned, suggesting that death was not caused by fire, and there is no sign of the usual burial practices. Here enters a crucial caveat, for the remains were not found in the state normally associated with the culture and time period, which involved what we might today call a decent burial. Therefore, the clues strongly imply an occurrence of survival cannibalism—which, although not unknown, was rare. The archeologists also point out that this particular era was one of climatic change and ecological disturbance in an already marginal economic environment which generated social unrest and conflict. All that can be deduced from the evidence is an isolated instance of man eating man among a group struggling to survive under harsh and unusual conditions. Needless to say, this does not permit the easy conclusion that the American Indians of the Southwest were gustatory or ritual cannibals. The peculiar circumstances of the

THE MAN-EATING MYTH

find actually suggest the opposite, since the normal way of disposing of the dead was not apparent.

Scattered throughout the archeological literature on the original settlers of North America one can find other examples hinting at further instances of cannibalism under stress conditions. The physical documentation is usually less conclusive than in the previous example, but the remains are in exceptional form, again indicating the absence of a cultural pattern (Hartman 1975). In general, the archeological reports are more modest and tentative, as might be expected where researchers are more accustomed to dealing with concrete artifacts capable of measurement and examination by more than one individual. Yet every so often someone inevitably falls victim to his own culture's myths. When such a publication makes its unmistakable appearance, it bears all the telltale marks of contemporary attitudes and mythology being forced on the past of mankind in the guise of Space Age science.

The Iroquois provide an apt setting for this sort of interpretative reporting, since popular media have already provided pre-set images which have some basis in fact. The members of the Iroquois confederation of the Northeast provide a striking contrast to the relatively pacific nature of many Southwestern Indians. The tribes of the loosely organized Iroquois confederation came into early and often sharp conflict with the first white settlers, due to the Indians' participation in the prized fur trade. They also became inextricably bound up in the economic competition and ensuing military clashes between the European powers on the scene. As a result, their bellicosity has gained a historical distinction which was not enhanced by the decision of some of the groups in the confederation to ally themselves with the British and Loyalists in the American War of Independence. Given this sort of tarnished reputation, they are often vilified in the historical and prehistoric literature. This attitude is illustrated by a recent essay on the Iroquois which originally appeared in a magazine for the non-specialist (Tuck 1974). Unfortunately, this opportunity to communicate with the general reading public all too often convinces an author of the necessity to jettison scientific standards along with jargon. This sort of patronizing attitude, more than anything else, is a disservice to both the readership and the discipline, not to mention the history of those who are the subject of the study.

In the expected vein, the supposed cannibalistic site in this instance has been dubbed "Bloody Hill." The area is located in the Onondaga region of New York State, near Syracuse, and the occupation dates to sometime around 1420 A.D. According to the reporter, the remains "yielded evidence that ritual torture and cannibalism, which were familiar in historical times, were an established part of the Iroquois culture in the 15th century" (Tuck 1974: 195). In one stroke of the pen, the Iroquois are rendered prehistoric and historic cannibals. However, the evidence is hardly sufficient for such a conclusion, for a single mysterious phenomenon leads the author to this proclamation. In the process of their extensive excavations, the archeological team uncovered one pit which had been used as an earth oven. Along with a few other refuse scraps which are not defined, the contents of the pit included the fragments of an adult male skull and long bones indicating cut marks. The accompanying photographs of the pit mention a "Savage Ritual" at which "evidently an adult male had been cooked and eaten" (192).

There are a number of valid specific and general objections to such a sensationalized account, which are implicit in earlier remarks. First, charred human remains do not necessarily imply that the remains were a repast. The individual might just as well have been cremated without being eaten. To the objection that the general archeological record does not indicate that the Iroquois cremated the dead, it can be countered that neither does the same record suggest cannibalism was a cultural pattern. Second, a singular instance such as this also rules out the use of the term "ritual," which in social-anthropological parlance has a restricted meaning. Importantly this concept implies the repetition of an act, not a one-time occurrence. It is likely that in the effort to provide a readable, familiar account, the author was not cognizant of this more technical meaning, but instead was attempting to convey another message by using the word "ritual" to imply an irrational supernatural motivation on the part of the Indians. There is a general tendency in much of the literature on "the natives" to define their actions as rituals, while our own behavior in contrast is called "customs," which implies a more rational purpose. Thus, in this example, a single instance of Iroquois activity, with no evidence on its possible meaning, is called the "Savage Ritual of Bloody Hill."

Finally, the historic record which the author alludes to in order to support his suspicions contains no first-hand account of Iroquois cannibalism. Despite wide acceptance of the notion about the Iroquois propensity to eat the heart of a stout brave they had just tortured to death, this is apparently another second-hand, time-worn myth. The collected documents of the Jesuit missionaries (Thwaites 1959), often referred to as the source for Iroquois cruelty and cannibalism, do not contain an eyewitness description of the latter deed. Accounts which reduce the American Indians to mindless savages are understandable in the context of sixteenth-century missionary reporting, but they deserve no place in the record of contemporary archeology.

This review of the eons preceding written history calls for one last digression into the past on the trail of the cannibal which evokes a brief consideration of a contemporary intellectual to-do focusing on the very origins of man's nature. Specifically, are *Homo sapiens* beastly—which everyone concerned seems to agree upon—because of genetic or because of cultural make-up? This question, which has a respected ancient lineage, has received new impetus from the modern descendants in the field of ethology or animal behavior. Sociobiology, which attempts to integrate the accumulated wisdom of the ages from various intellectual branches, is now becoming fashionable. This new synthesis also has something to say about why man eats man, which is seen as the ultimate in human nastiness. Since this new discipline rests upon only the very little that is known in the quest for the vast unknown, rampant human cannibalism is merely assumed. Almost every other question is open to debate—as the true believers of each persuasion draw the battle lines.

Each side passionately declares that we will make little intellectual or moral progress unless its opponents recognize the true nature of human aggression. Only their shared pessimism on the human condition provides a common meeting-ground, as both the civilized and primitive come in for a vigorous lambasting. As one crusader sums up the situation, "Indeed, the extreme nature of human destructiveness and cruelty is one of the principal characteristics which marks off man, behaviorally, from other animals" (Freeman 1964: 111). He then writes: "The history of primitive peoples with their bizarre expressions of human cruelty and aggression, in sacrificial rites, ceremonies of initiation, ritual mutilations, head-hunting and cannibalistic cults and murderous societies" (112–13) confirms this view of human nature. This is not a pretty picture to contemplate, but what is to be done? While one side claims we are at least partially genetically programmed in this direction, the other suggests that these are learned cultural responses. The proponents claim alike that their antagonists are peddling a dangerous fiction.

When the topic of cannibalism as a form of aggressiveness comes in for scrutiny, the debate becomes even more eloquent, for little else is capable of stirring the romantic incautious nature of the scientist. The anatomist Raymond Dart, who adopts the instinctive hypothesis and accepts the veracity of all reports on cannibalism from Strabo through Marco Polo to their nineteenth-century counterparts, writes, "The blood-bespattered, slaughter-gutted archives of human history . . . accord with early universal cannibalism" (Dart 1953: 207). Even Wilson, the grand synthesizer with a major academic investment in the notion of adapted aggressive instincts, refers to Dart's fulminations as "dubious anthropology, ethnology, and genetics" (1975: 255). He points out to the unwary who might stray too far in one direction that cannibalism is exhibited by a variety of other species in addition to man (246–47). This offers even further confirmation for the idea of an innate cannibalistic nature, for if only man-like creatures engaged in this practice, then the cultural component might take on a more important explanatory role. The argument demands that man the beast remain conspicuously in the foreground of the scene.

On the other side the reader encounters the rationale that cultural responses to various situations have produced a potential cannibalistic nature in man. Instead of the chromosomes, the heart and mind sometimes, sadly, demanded that our forebears eat each other in the past. Montagu, the standard-bearer of these forces, states that the ban on cannibalism is often only a "civilized prejudice" (1976: 111). Therefore, if civilized man has been able to shed the anthropophagic cloak in making moral progress, cannibalism or its denial is no more than a cultural feat. If we have been able to make this great leap forward while remaining members of the same species as the uncivilized, then there is hope for all to achieve the same level. Cannibalism is rendered nothing more than a backward trait. If the argument were to make its stand on this reasonable and defensible position, there would be little to which to object. However, as we have constantly observed, the cannibal has a great fascination for the academic mind, as this horrible creature demands further exculpation until every potential explanation has had its day. Not content to counter the sociobiologists with the proposal of cannibalism as a cultural expression of aggression, some demand that we recognize the hidden but real significance of cannibalism. It is a token of respect, if not true love.

Although a few others have dabbled with this hypothesis, Helmuth (1973) has given the motivational question the most extensive thought in recent times. His main concern in his review of the reported instances of man-eating from all eras and parts of the world is determining the modes of thought which underlie cannibalistic practices. He assumes that, by understanding the consciousness of more contemporary anthropophagists, we can arrive at some better understanding of what might have been going through the head of prehistoric man as he forced open the skull of his dead colleague in order to feast on the brain. Helmuth's essay has all the hallmarks of serious scholarship—extensive bibliography, tables, charts and statistical formulae to measure the relationship between economic base and type of cannibalism indulged in by South American Indians resulting in the most complex classificatory system yet to be encountered. However, the validity of the ethnographic data base is never questioned. Instead, in the rush to undermine the genetic aggressive position of the opposing school of thought, cannibalism is assumed as a given of the argument. He concludes with the safe proposition that the numerous different types of rationales he has uncovered in his research, which have motivated the world's many man-eaters, do not permit any monocausal interpretation for their behavior. To name just a few of the more intriguing types, the author proposes the existence of juridical, magical-ceremonial and funerary cannibalism. Furthermore, these and other motivations for the deed are delicately symbolized on a world map of anthropophagic locations by skulls, crossed daggers, coffins, urns, saucepans and scales of justice (246–47). Helmuth also demonstrates that the imagination necessary to do justice to the topic is rarely lacking.

Prophetically, Helmuth states that the assumption of cannibalism as an aggressive act is only an example of the application of contemporary moral notions on the human past. He writes that it would be feasible to argue that a primitive South American Indian practicing endocannibalism, which he renders even more obscurely as "patrophagy," "could imply a long history of friendly, loving feelings and affection" (250). With such scholarly apologists as defenders, the contemporary South American Indians need no enemies in the struggle to prevent the extermination of their way of life, for the bottom line always admits that they are or were man-eaters.

The reading matter on prehistoric cannibalism is fairly extensive, so it is not possible to do justice to all reports in this single chapter. However, the few examples cited above in some detail illustrate intellectual patterns and permit some general conclusions on the present state of mind and expertise of contemporary surveyors of the past. Although some may be improvident in their interpretation of the prehistoric evidence, by and large they are much more cautious in drawing conclusions than their colleagues who study historic and contemporary non-western societies. In a similar fashion, rash initial suggestions about cannibalism in former ages which spring to the surface in this field have been checked by cautionary remarks, if not countervailing interpretations. Stricter scholarly standards may have something to do with this condition, but equally significant is the existence of observable concrete artifacts. Not all of these conveniently disappear or retreat from view, as have the presumed living representations of cannibalism, so that the judgments of one individual, no matter how fantastic, do not have to be taken on faith by others interested in the same question. This ability to examine, test, and then retest the evidence as more refined methodological techniques become available has much to do with the guarded tenor of the reflections on prehistoric man. In contrast, the social anthropologist who spends time in an isolated area and returns to report that "his natives" formerly resorted—or even more excitingly, still resort—to cannibalism in secret does not have to face the same methodological testing by his colleagues. If anything, in order not to be outdone, others of the same frame of mind feel the need to claim that their people also did or do the same. Anthropologists and anthropophagists make strange but comfortable bedfellows; but elucidation of the reasons for this marriage awaits the arguments of the final chapter.

Indeed the archeologists and paleontologists arrive at some of their more indefensible deductions by their unsuspecting reliance on the contributions of social anthropologists whose research methods are not as rigorous. This suits the social anthropologists, whose ideas are then validated by those in allied fields by a circuitous feedback system of misinformation. Illustrating this process, two philosophically oriented students of early man, who were aware of the clues for cannibalism, attempted to reconstruct prehistoric ideologies by relying on the musings of social anthropologists who have reported similar behavior for twentieth-century primitive man (Bergounioux 1961 and Blanc 1961). Thus Bergounioux writes, "we are forced to make use of observations made on archaic peoples, who seem to us the only ones who kept the thought processes of very early man." (1961: 116). So simplistic a correlation is inviting, but not at all convincing. For example, Montagu, who has constantly maintained a cautious, scholarly position on the subject of cannibalism, has seriously undermined the entire evolutionary perspective. He points out that reports of cannibalism for more recent times are almost non-existent on hunting-gathering peoples, who have the simplest known economic system of adaption (1976: 111). This means that it is not possible to posit a relationship between primitive man and cannibalism as an atavistic aggressive trait, as many have done.

Having reviewed some of the most prominent finds and interpretations of those most intimately concerned with the behavior of prehistoric man, we can now return to the original topic of the evidence for cannibalism in the dim past. Taken as a whole, the rarity of the finds, including those of a dubious nature, does not permit the conclusion that the material evidence ever points to cannibalism as a cultural pattern in either gustatory or ritual form, in earlier times. This may come as a shock to the layman and popularizer, but it is apparent from the literature that this lack of a data base is not recognized by contemporary social anthropology, either. Whether through ignorance or misinterpretation of the facts, social anthropologists prefer to maintain in print and lecture that archeologists have uncovered almost as many cannibals in the past as they themselves have located in the modern era. However, this is far from the truth.

Finally, it is possible—and does no damage to the thesis of this book—to conclude that some of the remains in question suggest rare, isolated instances of prehistoric beings who engaged in survival cannibalism. It would be unreasonable to conclude that in the two-million-year history of man, such an attempt at survival would not have been resorted to by some. Most of the world's humans for most of their history have lived in marginal economic zones without sufficient technological systems to stave off disaster in its starkest expressions. Death by starvation under stress conditions must have been a familiar companion of early man. In this light, it is surprising that there have not been more archeological indications of our species resorting to cannibalism. The lack of such evidence might well indicate that the majority at any time has always felt the denial of human flesh to be a "civilized prejudice" and deemed the loss of life more agreeable than eating it.

V

THE
MYTHICAL WORLD
OF ANTHROPOPHAGY

The previous survey of selected cases has undoubtedly omitted someone's favorite cannibals from other times and places. To such a charge I can only plead that it would be impossible to examine each and every instance of reported cannibalism, since the unvarnished implication of the literature is that the act is or has been a cultural universal. As indicated, a strict interpretation of the material would necessarily include our own culture in this category. This profusion of cases has prompted the analysis of some of the most popular and best-documented case studies of cannibalistic societies. The guiding assumption has been that the best way to confront a popular set of images is to demonstrate the weaknesses of the best available evidence. Failure to take such an approach only invites continued doubts and suspicions.

On the other hand, continuing to assess the credibility of these literary accounts fails to make a positive contribution to our understanding of other cultures in general or of the specific question of man-eating. More importantly, proceeding in such a negative vein sustains a false and distracting issue. Continued inquests on the rationale for what drove man to eat his colleagues have already initiated learned yet sterile paper wars, reminiscent of nineteenth-century scholarship. The most certain thing to be said is that all cultures, subcultures, religions, sects, secret societies and every other possible human association have been labeled anthropophagic by someone. In this light, the contemporary, though neglected, anthropological problem emerges more clearly. The idea of "others" as cannibals, rather than the act, is the universal phenomenon. The significant question is not why people eat human flesh, but why one group invariably assumes that others do. Accounting for a single aspect of an overall system of thought, rather than an observable custom, becomes the issue.

Moving in this direction allows for the evaluation of further common evidence for cannibalism, but the material can now be interpreted in a more positive way. The process also has something to contribute to our understanding of human imagination and culture, including our own. This facet of the problem was shelved in the previous search for gaps, errors, inconsistencies, and other related shortcomings of particular published accounts. Many of the ideas to be developed in the following pages have been implicit in previous ones; but a more systematic development of them is required in order to consider how a particular idea gains acceptability and becomes part of common knowledge in our culture as well as in others. This second basic concern of this inquiry often means abandoning the realm of formal scholarship for the arena of ordinary notions about human behavior. However, the shift in orientation is not very demanding, since in some instances the primary boundary between the esoteric and pedestrian modes of thought is nothing more than a technical vocabulary. Very often the illiterate and the literati share similar unfounded ideas about human behavior.

In examining the pervasiveness of the notion of others as cannibals, the implication that this charge denies the accused their humanity is immediately recognizable. Defining them in this way sweeps them outside the pale of culture and places them in a category with animals (cf. Clerk 1975: 3). "Those" people, whether they inhabit the next valley or another continent, lack culture because human beings do not eat each other. Eating human flesh succinctly signals an individual or group as nonhuman in a basic way. In many cultures, the human body is potentially the most sacred symbol (Douglas 1970), so that the act of eating human flesh becomes the most profane act imaginable unless conducted in the context of a highly charged symbolic event.

The fact that only those animals who somehow invert their own natural order, such as the renegade lion or tiger and certain

species such as the solitary nocturnal leopard or hyena, sometimes prey on humans for food strengthens the symbolic association between cannibalism and antisocial behavior. Other species
which in some way subvert the human interpretation of the
natural order of things, such as the alligator, a reptile which
inhabits the arena of fish, and the baboon, who physically paro-
dies man and invades his domain for food, become other potential
markers of evil. These are also the very species which human
beings often exclude from their diet whenever possible because of
their unsavory nature. Consequently there are many groups in
Africa usually included on the list of cannibals who refuse to
include baboon meat on their menu because these animals are
thought to be too reminiscent of people—an attitude that would
seem to imply a concomitant aversion to human flesh itself.
These animal imitations of the human form and categorical
affronts to the intellect are then assumed to prey on ordinary
humans in some supernatural form. It is no coincidence that in
Sierra Leone and other parts of Africa suspected cannibals are
thought to take the shape of human leopard, baboon and alligator societies. Lacking such environmental opportunities, our own
literary and folk traditions propose the wolf and bat as the symbols of such evil, and assume that humans who lust after the
bodily substances of their own kind would choose this bestial
form.

Such subtle symbolic associations are meaningful, but often
only in obscure and restricted ways. Branding whole groups as
cannibals is much more to the point and obvious to all concerned.
Warfare and annihilation are then excusable, while more sophisticated forms of dominance, such as enslavement and colonization, become an actual responsibility of the culture-bearers. Half
of the world's people have been saved from their own or their
neighbors' worst inclinations in this way. Poignant quotes from
the self-congratulatory reflections of the agents of western civilization about the base nature of their charges are readily available.

However, this discourse is concerned with the general capability of the human mind, not particular moral lapses, so it is better to go further afield.

Ironically, no sentiment more adequately expresses this notion of others as cannibals than some advice offered to Mead in New Guinea as she prepared to leave the Arapesh for the Mundugumor. In what must have been the somberest of tones, her Arapesh informant warned her: "You are going up the Sepik River, where the people are fierce, where they eat men. . . . We are another kind. So you will find it" (1950: 165). She did not find it, returned safely without ever observing the act, but managed to effectively communicate this bit of sage counsel about cannibals to the outside world. Given the time and effort, it might be possible to trace the path of such accusations in an unbroken chain across an entire continent. For example, the Baganda who live on the shores of Lake Victoria claim that inhabitants of the Sese Islands of this vast inland sea eat interlopers. The Sese deny this, but admit that the natives on the far shore are indeed cannibals. Unfortunately, the material trails off at this point, since the ethnographer failed to check with the latest suspects (Johnston 1902: 693).

The anthropologist, whose function is to be more aware of cultural boundaries underlying such accusations, should be able to assess this sort of information critically. This has not been the case, as such expressions of prejudice on the part of non-westerners are instead accepted as evidence for cannibalism. It is not surprising therefore that non-specialists who tend to paint the world in broader strokes would accept this as firm documentation, since they tend to see all the natives of an area as one type. However, this is not a realistic appraisal of human nature. A New Guinean or African group is as prone to debase another with the cannibal label as quickly as any European.

A second instructive example of this sort is provided by Francis Huxley, who conducted his fieldwork among the Urubu

Indians of Brazil, the contemporary remnants of a broad culture group which included the infamous Tupinamba. These representatives of an all-but-extinct culture were no longer cannibals, according to the author, since they had been brought under administrative control some twenty-five years earlier. Yet Huxley was well aware of their prior savage nature from his grasp of the literature written on the Tupinamba and related peoples by earlier commentators. As a result, he badgered his informants to provide him with some contemporary ethnographic detail on this former practice. In his popularly written monograph, he unabashedly states: "Of cannibalism it is almost impossible to get them to talk: a direct question brings out merely a bored and aloof denial" (1957: 234). One of his best friends and informants responded with disgust at the very idea, but, undeterred, the author adds that this was not at all convincing. Then the ethnographer, whose purpose was to collect material on their traditional culture, turned the table on the Indians and proceeded to show and tell them the truth about themselves.

He was assisted in the task by an illustrated traveler's account of the area's residents in the nineteenth century. Turning to a picture of some neighboring Apiaca, Huxley casually informed his new students of western anthropology that these Indians used to eat people. "Eat people!" one native exclaimed, "this book's no good, throw it in the fire" (235). This of course only confirmed the instructor's suspicions. Consequently, he then turned to a drawing of the Munduruku Indians: "'They also ate people,' I said, to stimulate him, though it was quite untrue" (235). His best student finally took the bit between his teeth and then admitted this to be the "sad" truth of the matter. The same individual proceeded to identify all the other Indians depicted in the manuscript in the same fashion. He concluded: "White men are always telling us that we ate people, that we ate whites. It's a lie, we didn't. We didn't eat people. Never! [The] Juru pihun ate people, but we're good, we didn't" (236). The informant then added the

Capiwan to the now rapidly growing list of cannibals who formerly preyed on the ancestors of the Urubu.

Huxley then seized the opportunity to tell his Indian listeners he had heard an account of how the Capiwan formerly killed and ate people. As if it did not matter, in a casual aside to the reading audience, he says: "The account was really that of Tupinamba cannibalism." His informant again confirmed the story, and then related a detailed myth of Capiwan cannibalism. The author took this to be a projection of what the Urubu actually did themselves but would not admit to. He concludes this chapter with the astounding phrase that the story, "though a piece of history, can also be read as a myth" (243). Thus the Urubu and related Indians were confirmed by contemporary anthropology as former anthropophagists. Admittedly, social anthropology can never be a science in the same sense as other disciplines. Yet there is legitimate reason to expect more in terms of a scientific method in the way that data are accumulated, presented and interpreted. In light of the account frankly admitted to by Huxley, one wonders what his informants would have had to say to stave off this characterization. The definition of the Urubu as cannibals is as historically inevitable as their eventual extinction at the hands of the civilized.

Ironically, Thomas H. Huxley, the nineteenth-century anthropologist and the contemporary Huxley's great-grandfather, had a hand in transmitting the notion of African cannibalism to the western world. In one of his many publications, in a postscript to a chapter on African apes, he provided a traveler's account of Congo cannibalism and selected a sixteenth-century print to illustrate the horrid scene. The image portrays a smiling Congolese butcher preparing human cutlets in his outdoor shop (1898: 74). The elder Huxley accepted the veracity of this material without commentary. However, in response to the same traveler's observations on the man-like apes of Central Africa, the scientific mind re-emerges. Just prior to moving on to the subject of cannibalism, Huxley concludes his treatment of the data on apes with the comment: "It may be truth, but it is not evidence" (72). The same might be said of his great-grandson's tales from the jungles of Brazil in the twentieth century.

Accepting Francis Huxley's informants' statements on their cannibalistic neighbors at face value would be unforgivably naive in other contexts. In form and function, these remarks are analogous to those offered Mead about other natives living near her New Guinea informants. Taken together with a score of other examples, this suggests that we are dealing, in part at least, with an instance of collective prejudice. This attitude is not a unique western failing, since it finds expression wherever there are two human groups in contact. In a more technical parlance, the assumption by one group about the cannibalistic nature of others can be interpreted as an aspect of cultural-boundary construction and maintenance. This intellectual process is part of the attempt by every society to create a conceptual order based on differences in a universe of often-competing neighboring communities. In other words, one group can appreciate its own existence more meaningfully by conjuring up others as categorical opposites. This may be difficult to accomplish when the groups share similar cultural patterns, so the differences must often be invented. What could be more distinctive than creating a boundary between those who do and those who do not eat human flesh? In effect, this means a line is drawn between the civilized and savage modes of existence, which translate as "we" and "they." As disappointing as it may be, we are not the only people in this world to claim a monopoly on culture. In great dismay but with little reluctance, people everywhere point the finger at their barbaric, cannibalistic neighbors.

This attitude may be meaningful to those who hold it so dearly, but by itself such an idea would prove insufficient to prop up such an elaborate civilized cosmology as that attending on the cannibal notion. There is more in the way of less ephemeral evidence, and it is time to consider some of the more obvious cultural clues which have led to the assumption of cannibalism on the part of so many of the world's people.

The belief that others are or were cannibals is enhanced by the familiar fact that the people in question often cherish a myth about an obscure "once-upon-a-time" past, which includes an account of eating human flesh. These stories pinpoint the emergence of their culture from a pre-civilized stage by recounting the deletion of human flesh from the food category. The Chamula Indians of Mexico provide an interesting case, because their ideas exemplify how the fringes of time and space are brought together when cannibalism is being considered. The Chamula share a common mythical structure of worldwide distribution which includes creation of humans and later their destruction for the commission of unpardonable sins. They look upon the present as the fourth re-creation, and explain the demise of the inhabitants of the first stage as being caused by their custom of eating their own children. Having told the anthropologist of this, some of the Indians wanted to know if people still ate each other where the researchers hailed from in faraway California (Gossen 1975).

In addition to being widespread, these stories also often contain the common element of making reference to incest in explicit or symbolic form (cf. Lévi-Strauss 1969). There are two reasons for this equation. First, like eating human flesh, incest is a striking indication of a lack of culture. As a result, cannibals were also accused of having no incest taboo. Subsequent investigations by professional anthropologists, with their interest in kinship and marriage systems, have laid this myth to rest. Second, in many cultures, including ours, there is a symbolic equation between sex and eating. Consequently, cannibalism in the mythical past, as among the Chamula, often takes the form of one member of the family devouring another as the ultimate horror. There are many cultures in which folklore takes up this theme, but none more elaborate and instructive than our own, as retold by Freud in

Totem and Taboo. As if incest and cannibalism were insufficient markers of a pre-cultural stage, a dash of patricide is added, as the offspring kill and eat their father for hoarding the females. In a subsequent state of remorse, they put incest and cannibalism behind them and set out on the road to civilization. Freud refers to the event as "this memorable and criminal deed, which was the beginning of many things—of social organization, of moral restrictions and of religion" (1950: 142). In effect, morality, in the form of human as opposed to animal social organization, as evidenced by the taboos on incest and cannibalism, was invented in one swift stroke.

The absence of breakdown of culture which the human mind often finds a satisfying notion to contemplate can be portrayed in the same fashion. This technique was recently epitomized in the low-budget and rather amateurish film *"The Night of the Living Dead,* which despite disparaging critical reviews has become a contemporary cult film. In one gruesome scene the director turns back Freud's calendar to the pre-cultural stage as a young girl is transformed into a ghoul and then begins to dine on her mother. Thus in a single instance the taboos on incest, lesbianism and cannibalism are violated in either explicit or symbolic form. The critics, who are very often more concerned with technique than content, have been genuinely amazed and dismayed by the film's attraction. However, they do not realize that the film is true horror in the sense of riveting the viewer's attention on something which is prohibited but nonetheless fascinating to consider. Such a scene as the one described implies total human freedom by depicting the absence of the strongest and most elementary social constraints, which include the prohibition on human flesh.

To return to Freud's mythical reconstruction, we may recognize how it also implies that culture was a masculine product whose regulations were then imposed on females who—as in much of Freud's deliberations—only emerge as passive figures. Although not immediately pertinent, this last facet of the tale does point out that we are dealing with little more than a culturally acceptable fabrication having as little bearing on empirical reality as a horror film.

As the natives in this instance, we realize the absurdity of accepting such figurative reconstructions of an unknowable past or representations of horror as literal truth. However, early visitors to many parts of the world where similar visions prevail either intentionally or unintentionally failed to distinguish between allegory and description. Regrettably, these misconceptions have filtered into contemporary anthropology as substantiation for cannibalism immediately prior to the arrival of the first Westerner or fieldworker. The situation is comparable to some alien recorder of western culture concluding that we were once cannibals since the theme emerges explicitly in Greek mythology and, only thinly disguised, in less profound fairy-tales such as "Sleeping Beauty," "Hansel and Gretel," and "Jack and the Beanstalk," to mention only a few examples.

Consequently, a contemporary anthropologist (Levy 1973) is able to state that

Reports of pre-Christian Tahiti indicate that another symbolic aspect of eating was the question of being eaten oneself. The Tahitians were not cannibals at the time of European discovery, but their neighbors in the Tuamotus and Marquesas were . . . and their traditions indicated that they had been in the past. A vocabulary of cannibalism persisted. The missionary Ellis noted as examples of insults, "mayst thou be baked as food for thy mother" and "take out your eyeball and give it to your neighbor to eat." . . . one of the phrases which designated incest was, and still is . . . "to eat people," which was also the term for cannibalism [107–8].

In addition to exemplifying almost every aspect of the problem so far discussed, the ethnographic detail makes the direct equation between incest and cannibalism by employing a single term for both socially disapproved acts. This is a common theme in the area (Fischer et al. 1976 and Labley 1976). The Yapese, who share some of our notions, expect such behavior from New Guineans, whom they say are cannibals, but not themselves. Like Freud, they make it explicit that incest and cannibalism are forms of survival through "self-consumption" and the denial of culture (Labley 1976: 171). In light of our present appreciation of origin myths and folklore, it is difficult to understand how this sort of information could be interpreted as historical evidence for cannibalism; yet it is a common enough conclusion.

To this point the reader has had little opportunity to consider in original and complete form the material which has been reinterpreted in this study as failing to provide adequate documentation for cannibalism. The Azande, who were, as indicated, famous African cannibals, provide a text on the subject which in its translated form is presented in full below. This provides a brief opportunity to evaluate the material without an intermediary.

"In the past Azande were just like animals of the bush, because they killed people and ate their fellows just like lions, leopards, and wild dogs. In the past when a man died a Zande sharpened his knife, moved over to the corpse, and cut off the flesh, about two basketfuls of it, and went home with this flesh to his home. He took a very big pot and placed the human flesh in it till it was filled, and then he put it on the fire. It stewed for a long time, then he took it off the fire to take it to a drying platform over a fire to dry. He took it from there and cooked it in his pot by himself. That pot he used for eating human flesh, another man would not touch it in any circumstances, it was kept apart by itself always, only he himself touched it. His fireplace was by itself on one side. When he was of a mind to eat his man he lit his fire by himself at the base of some tree, and he took his dried human flesh, some three or four pieces of it, and put them on the fire (in a pot), and he closed the mouth of the pot with another little pot. It went on stewing till it was cooked; meanwhile his wife ground sesame for him to go with it. He did all the cooking (of the meat) himself. His wife cooked porridge and gave it to him by the side of his flesh. He ate his porridge and his flesh till he was satisfied, and then he covered over the mouth of the pot and put it at the side of the granary till he was hungry again. Azande used to say that they ate a man because he made good meat. A Zande used to say in the old days thus, 'What was a stranger to him?' Since it was a stranger he would eat him up entirely because he was meat. But that business of eating people, it really began with forebears, that man whose forebear ate men before, he himself ate them when he grew up. It is thus in truth that Azande used to eat people in the past. Those clans who used to eat people in the past, as Kuagbiaru himself witnessed, were the Akpura, the Agiti, the Abamburo, and many other clans besides. For in the past almost all Azande used to eat people. Those who did not eat people used to think of those that ate people as lions, leopards, hyaenas, and wild dogs. They were afraid of those who used to eat people, saying that they might eat themselves also. They were in the eyes of men repulsive, horrible people; others made fun of them mockingly on account of their eating human flesh. When they came to court, the young warriors gathered around them to ask them about it; since they ate people how did they go about it to eat them? Everybody gathered around them to look at them'' [Evans-Pritchard 1956: 73–74].

There is little need to belabor the reader with the obvious. Suffice it to say this is not an eyewitness account on the part of the storyteller or the translator; it refers to an unspecified time in the past; it equates the alleged cannibals with carnivorous animals as non-humans and finally indicates that the idea of cannibalism is "repulsive" and "horrible" to the people. In sum, the text provides no substantiation for the belief that the Azande were man-eaters prior to European contact, but it does demonstrate many of the characteristics of the evidence which have come in for commentary in this chapter.

Another explanation for the pervasiveness of the idea of cannibalism is also closely related to the failure to distinguish between an exotic culture's view of the supernatural and its view of the natural world. Although every society makes such a distinction, casual sojourners with little if any competence in the local language have been unable to detect what we know to be an often subtle native boundary between reality and fantasy. This failure explains those literary accounts which explain that informants frankly and voluntarily admitted there were some people among themselves who indulged in human flesh. The result has been the accumulation of massive evidence on cannibalism, but often the material leaves something to be desired as documentation for actual behavior.

For example, the widespread assumption of the cannibalistic nature of the American Indians of northeastern Canada is based in large part on their myths and still-extant belief about man-eating giants who stalk forlorn forests of the area. However, this is more than a local variation of "Jack and the Beanstalk," since the idea of cannibalism in various guises is a dominant cultural theme. As Teichler demonstrates, under aboriginal conditions the natives of this desolate area were involved in a precarious relationship with their harsh environment to the extent that survival was never a foregone conclusion. As a result, stories and rumors of cannibalism were rife as an indication of some hunting bands having reached the last resort in the struggle for survival. More than dreading others, theirs was an anxious, personal fear that they would be forced to revert to this savage act themselves if the hunt failed. Therefore, it is likely that survival cannibalism actually occurred, but it is even more apparent that such an eventuality was looked upon with the utmost repugnance by the Indians. As Teichler points out in his meticulous essay, there was no pattern of ritual cannibalism or related behavior in any socially approved form. Indeed, faced with the choice of cannibalism or death, they often chose the latter (1960: 16).

However, the story does not end here, for the aboriginal northeast is famous in the literature of psychological anthropology for the occurrence of the "windigo psychosis." This aberration was characterized by an individual's compulsive desire to eat human flesh which could be satisfied by the "windigo" actually attacking members of his own family, again implying the violation of the incest taboo. Needless to say, the act was not condoned, and the killing of such a deviant individual by the community was considered to be a regrettable act of self-defense, since he was a constant threat to normal social intercourse. Teichler (1960: 5) also adds that the sufferer would even request that someone take his life rather than allowing him to continue to exist in this deplorable condition. The Indians provided a number of explanations for this bizarre behavior, including the assumption that the victim of the illness had once secretly tasted human flesh out of necessity and could no longer be satisfied by any other meat. Whatever the cause, there was general agreement that such a condition was lamentable and an abnormal emotional state whose expression was shaped by particular traditional cultural themes. Such psychotic states still make their appearance today among these Indians, but no longer fixate on the desire for human flesh. On this basis some might suggest that cannibalism has died out in this area, but such a hypothesis would be rendered absurd by the foregoing evidence.

An additional bizarre, but at least light-hearted, example of evidence for cannibalism has been supplied by a colleague who lived among an East African group with a widespread reputation among their neighbors for cannibalism. The dialogue as reported is as follows:

Anthropologist:	Your people have a reputation for eating human flesh. Is there any truth in this story?
Informant:	None whatsoever.
Anthropologist:	There are no cannibals among you?
Informant:	That's true.
Anthropologist:	Are you sure—not even one?
Informant:	Well, there is one.
Anthropologist:	Who?
Informant:	My brother-in-law. He's giving the rest of us a bad name.

Unfortunately, little of the other data bearing on cannibalism has this amusing air or the timing so suspiciously similar to a Marx Brothers exchange, but often the quality is the same. According to the informants from New Guinea to Africa, those who are accused of being cannibals by their fellows are also witches. Actually, it would be better to say that the accused are first and foremost witches, who engage in cannibalism as only one of their many antisocial tendencies. They also have the amazing ability to fly through the night, become invisible, change into animals and kill their victims by merely wishing for the event. Often they consume their victims in such a mystical fashion that others do not notice what has transpired. In one example from New Guinea, the victim is no more aware of what is happening than is the object of a vampire's attention, who in our classic tale of horror slowly expires, despite the ministrations of both medical and folk science. After some passing references to cannibalism, the author provides the following passage, which appears to be a direct translation of native statements:

The sorceress attacks at night when her victim is asleep, or in the day when you do not notice. . . . The sorceress strikes you with a stone adze; when you fall down unconscious she eats your flesh, then leaves you. You wake up remembering nothing and go about your activities as usual—then you become ill and die [Barth 1975: 132].

In addition to being a physical impossibility, in the way in which we view the natural universe, this and similar visions are reflections of a nightmare world. Thus the implication is clear that, if cannibalism were ever actually to take place, eating human flesh would be looked upon as an abhorred activity, rather than a condoned custom. The failure to comprehend that they were dealing with inverted moral orders, rather than descriptions of concrete happenings, has led some non-anthropologists to arrive at absurd conclusions about "the savage mind." On the other hand, this same sort of evidence has led some anthropologists to consider the potential nutritional value of anthropophagy. In both camps, there has been the familiar selective sorting process as certain information is dismissed because it does not conform to established notions, while other bits are retained. To put it succinctly, we recognize that witches cannot exist because the evidence for such a phenomenon is scientifically untenable. We assume cannibals exist, but not because the act has been physically observed, since the evidence is lacking. The assumption therefore rests primarily on the accusations made by one group or individual against another.

The significance of the belief that members of a culture may hold about the existence of supernatural evil-doers who seek the flesh of others is difficult to grasp fully in the abstract. Fortunately, Winter's (1963) exposition of Amba witchcraft as a system of thought permits a more meaningful appreciation of the subject. The Amba are typical Bantu agriculturalists straddling the border between Uganda and Zaire in Central Africa. Their location was enough to earn them an honored place on the roll of cannibals, but their peculiar portrayal of the supernatural world lent further credence to this belief. Like many other African groups, the Amba believe that personal misfortune is visited upon them by witches who during the day appear as normal individuals but at night transform themselves into malevolent supernatural beings. The primary purpose of these witches is to kill their unwary victims for the sake of human flesh, which they then consume in a mystical fashion so that the corpse shows no outward sign of having been touched. Although the Amba accept the existence of such creatures, the actions of witches with their unnatural craving for the flesh of their fellow man are considered reprehensible.

The basic antisocial character of these ghoulish fiends is exemplified by considering the full range of Amba thought on this matter. According to this belief system, witches are active at night, go about naked, can transform themselves into animals, eat salt when thirsty, choose their victims from among their co-villagers who are also their kinsmen, work in harmony with witches from other villages, and finally hang upside down from the limbs of trees. The last feature, which is clearly the least obnoxious trait, is also the most obvious clue to the thought pattern because it concretely illustrates that witches are believed to have constructed and to inhabit an inverted physical and moral universe. As Winter explains, the Amba hold that normal people are active during the day, would be ashamed to appear naked, cannot take on animal form and believe in peaceful cooperation with their neighbors and kinsmen, rather than Amba of other villages, who are their actual or potential enemies. Needless to say, the typical Amba drinks water when thirsty, is unable to hang head down from tree limbs and detests the idea of human meat.

This thought pattern allows for two straightforward conclusions: one, Amba witches, and therefore cannibals, exist only in the minds of their creators, and two, cannibalism is viewed as an aspect of the antisocial world, and thus would not be condoned any more than bloodsucking would be among those who have a remarkably similar belief structure about vampires. It should be reiterated that the Amba firmly believe in the existence of these enemies within their gates. Winter's biography (1959) of four Amba contains volunteered accounts by those who claim to have actually had horrible midnight confrontations with upside-down man-eaters. Therefore, it would be just as hopeless to try to convince these remote, illiterate Amba that cannibals do not really exist as it would be to dissuade their colleagues of a similar persuasion at the great intellectual institutions of the western world.

We have thus far one group accusing another of cannibalism or, more precisely, a group which admits to the existence of supernatural figures among them who have such leanings. Evidence of this type is not very substantial when considered in the proper social and cultural context which involves beliefs and accusations only, since no one has actually owned up to the deed. If this were the only type of documentation, it would be difficult to understand how the belief in others as cannibals could become so firmly entrenched. However, not all of the evidence is so patently flimsy, for as we have already seen in different times and places, for voluntary or involuntary reasons, some people have admitted to cannibalism. Many of these examples can be drawn from European incidents, as witches and heretics, because of torture or fear, confessed to the now-familiar pattern of cannibalism and incestuous orgies at their gatherings. Thus the church hierarchy made it abundantly clear that without the guidance of the church, people revert to a precultural, bestial form of behavior.

However, it is possible to draw on a more pertinent African example where cannibalism is still admitted to in this age for the sake of the rewards involved. This peculiar instance is provided by the Bangwa of West Africa, among whom, the anthropologist in charge writes, the confessions of "sky children," as their child witches are called, are always "very meaty" and "the meat is human" (Brain 1970: 173). He reports in some detail that, while he was in the field, a young boy confessed to his father that he and his playmates were witches who had been to the sky, where they had dined on his sister. As compensation for the boy's having owned up to this nefarious prank and, more importantly, for his promising to desist before it was too late, the father slaughtered a goat. At the feast which followed, he distributed the meat to all the children involved in the conspiracy. Shortly thereafter, the little girl who had been ill recovered.

The explanation provided by the author resolves this mystery with admirable facility. Among the Bangwa, he argues, the children are bribed by the promise of an offer of normally scarce meat to substantiate the adult world-view of supernatural evil. Further, as they do so, the children also begin to adopt the adult worldview. Whether or not they really believe in witches or in the actual occurrence of these events is irrelevant. Everyone, including the average six-year-old in our society, realizes Santa Claus does not bring the Christmas presents, but this has not meant the demise of the myth, for it has many uses. What is relevant, though, is that for the Bangwa, as for any other society, an explanation for the persistent occurrence of misfortune and evil is a necessity. This belief in the temporary transgressions of "sky children" fills the bill as well as any creature from the underworld.

Continuing with an examination of this intra-societal belief in cannibals inevitably leads to those accusations which clearly express the opposition between the sexes. In some social systems where this dichotomy is expressed in the form of patterned antagonistic beliefs, as among many New Guinea groups, the cannibal label is often attached to the women. Among the Hewa of New Guinea, who have generated this sort of system, it is held that the witches, who are all women, are motivated by their craving for human meat (Steadman 1975). Those suspected of witchcraft are often killed in the attempt to stop them from eventually murdering their victims, who are individuals actually suffering from an illness. Consequently more than simple sexist attitudes is at stake. In a rare moment of candor for the discipline, the anthropologist concerned is quick to point out that these homocides take place even though there is no evidence for actual cannibalism. The definition of women in this negative fashion is part of the general and pervasive cultural theme which views females as a source of danger or pollution to men. Further, the anthropologist adds that, by means of a system of food taboos, Hewa women are deprived of most animal protein. The males assume that, as a reaction to their domination and monopoly over this scarce resource, women would resort to cannibalism for the sake of meat and the desire for retribution. The outcome of this collective guilt and fear is the masculine belief that women are capable of performing the most depraved antisocial acts. This viewpoint is obviously passed on to every visitor, from missionary to medical officer, by the typical male informant. However, in this instance, the discerning interpreter was able to decipher the meaning of the belief system, rather than merely reporting in passing, as do many of his colleagues, that Hewa women were formerly cannibals.

As the previous examples indicate, in simpler societies, where the basic internal social divisions are between the generations or sexes, women and children are often cast as witches and cannibals by the dominant males (Lévi-Strauss 1975). Among peoples where kinship principles play a more significant organizational role, members of different clans, especially if systematic intermarriage is involved, are suspected of this sort of activity. In-laws are never to be trusted entirely in any society. With the most complex social systems, characterized by some form of internal division based upon the unequal distribution of wealth and/or power, the oppressed and oppressing classes view each other through a visor clouded by moral judgments. The poor and powerless are thought to be ignorant, lazy, dirty and to possess a host of other related characteristics. Such accusations are not easily hurled back at the privileged few, who are instead thought to revel in various forms of decadence beyond those of the simple folk. In this mode, one of Sahagún's informants, in one of the rare direct references to cannibalism, states that after sacrificing a slave at the pyramid, he was cooked and "then the nobility, and all the important men ate [the stew]; but not the common folk—only the leaders" (Sahagún 1951: 179).

The very same belief was held on the other side of the world by Fijian commoners about their aristocratic class. There are even recorded instances of the political elite attempting to use such suspicions as ideological props for their regime. This strategy involves hinting that the aristocracy consume human flesh and often also marry incestuously and calling upon the commoners to recognize their rulers as another order of beings who are not bound by conventional morality. As supernatural beings, they rule by dint of divinity, not human legitimacy (cf. Miller 1976: 242–51). Before dismissing this argument as an attempt to water down the evidence for cannibalism, recall that the common Africans held these very suspicions about their European colonial masters. On what basis is one native accusation to be ignored, while the other two are accepted as ethnographic fact? To us, the story of a member of the European nobility who preys on the blood of peasants is a compelling form of imagery with various symbolic overtones. Perhaps it would be best to view all stories of this type as folklore, rather than treating some from the non-European world as fact and some as folklore.

This review of the kind of material which has so often been carelessly used to support the contention of an almost worldwide countenance of cannibalism suggests that a basic re-ordering of the ethnographic data is called for. Classifying societies according to how they resort to man-eating in the sense of being endocannibals or exocannibals, ritual or gustatory cannibals would now appear to be a dubious intellectual exercise, since it lacks supporting evidence of the most basic kind. If there is a classificatory problem for those who feel a need to confront it, then the issue revolves around the question of how societies think about the phenomenon of cannibalism. Some groups reserve the category for neighboring societies. In this way, they define their sense of worth and draw the line between contemporary civilization and barbarism. Others may employ the idea as a mythic marker in the progress of their own cultural development. This involves postulating the eating of human flesh as a former social stage which has now been abandoned. Finally, the concept of cannibalism can be reserved for contemporary members of one's own society in the endeavor to explain the existence of constant evil and misfortune.

A categorical system of this order could easily be propounded, but it would involve an uncalled-for abuse of the language. Such an ordering device most often suggests that a problem has been solved merely because it is responsive to a mechanical intellectual process. Furthermore, the end result would be an artificial oversimplification. The idea of cannibalism is so attractive and useful that a single society can interpret the notion in numerous ways at the same or different times—depending upon the definitional problem at hand. The human mind is capable of generating extremely subtle symbolic messages which fortunately often defy the best efforts of those who seek to decode their structure. Some further brief examples illustrate the perplexing character of the problem of interpretation.

As suggested earlier, the idea of consuming the human body is often viewed as the most profane act imaginable. Consequently, all over the world, the fear of such a possibility is commonly used to express the most basic form of malevolence. However, by the paradox which is religion, in the sense that it often demands a suspension of everyday reasoning and standards, the very same notion of eating human flesh and blood is transformed into the most sacred of all acts. In this way, religious systems demonstrate their ideological superiority over other moral precepts and the human mind.

The idea of communion with the supernatural through a eucharistic feast is not commonplace, but neither is it the exclusive possession of Judeo-Christian thought. For example, Goody (1962) reports that for the Lo Dagga of West Africa, during the funeral ceremony, a steer is sacrificed in the name of the dead man. As this meat is eaten by the kin, they say it is the flesh of the deceased, rather than the animal. Further, as we know, much to the consternation of their European conquerors, the Aztecs also made edible images of their dieties for consumption at sacred rituals. Pointing out to those involved that actual flesh is not present is of little value, because the transformation is a mysterious event, beyond explanation.

Confronting this ingenuous symbolic facility of the mind is fraught with difficulties, as the attempt to comprehend the meaning of eucharistic communion in our culture demonstrates. A dismissal of this most meaningful Christian ritual as merely a conscious, mechanical, symbolic act on the part of the celebrants is confounded by the insistence of the true believer that the ordinary substances have become flesh and blood. In other words, the natives demand a strict rather than a symbolic interpretation of the act, which implies the ingestion of human flesh.

Mary Douglas points out that those contemporary Christian thinkers who have sought to interpret the Eucharist as a symbolic event have been rebuked *ex cathedra* by the Pope. In the encyclical *Mysterium Fidei*, issued in 1965, Paul warns the faithful that it would be spiritually fatal

to be so preoccupied with considering the nature of the sacramental sign that the impression is created that the symbolism—and no one denies its existence in the most holy Eucharist—expresses and exhausts the whole meaning of Christ's presence in this sacrament. Nor is it right to treat the mystery of transubstantiation without mentioning the marvellous change of the whole of the bread's substance into Christ's body and the whole of the wine's substance into his blood [quoted in Douglas 1970: 46–47].

As Douglas comments, these words are as uncompromising as those of any non-Christian fetishist on the score of the physical presence of the deity (47).

In light of this perplexing ability of the human intellect to demand the suspension of intellectual activity, it is not really difficult to understand how so many people have become convinced that other cultures actually engage in cannibalism. If representatives of such cultures collectively or selectively admit to consuming flesh in secret and sacred rituals, then only a certain turn of mind would deny the most obvious conclusions that those in question are cannibals. However, it is exactly this turn of mind which we have a right to expect from those who claim the specialized ability to understand rather than merely haphazardly report on other cultures.

The journey through the world of man-eaters has often been torturous, but we have finally reached the point where we can best appreciate the anthropological contribution and role in the "cannibal complex." This final discourse is called for because there is more involved than a close correspondence between the way in which the two words are spelled and pronounced. Anthropology and anthropophagy, as views of the external world, have had a comfortable and supportive relationship. It is possible that in their present form one could not exist without the other.

VI

THE
MYTHICAL WORLD
OF ANTHROPOLOGY

The material considered in the previous chapters clearly shows that anthropologists have made no serious attempt to disabuse the public of the widespread notion of the ubiquity of anthropophagists. The few excursions in this general direction, characterized by a careful scrutiny of the evidence and guarded conclusions (cf. de Mortillet 1886 and Montagu 1937), have languished in obscurity. It would be more apt to say that these endeavors have been buried under a mass of more sensational reports which intensify the extent and notion of man-eaters. Neither the producers nor the consumers of ideas are attracted by the possibility of diminishing the number of cannibals or incidence of cannibalism. The obvious preference runs in the direction of transforming those suspected of being cannibals into confirmed ritual endocannibals and then, in the twentieth century, into gustatory exocannibals on a grand scale. The Aztec case is a classic example of this trend, which took on momentum without the accumulation of additional evidence on the act itself. The idea and image of cannibalism expands with time and the intellectual appetite. Only the fleeting quality of the documentation remains constant.

In the deft hands and fertile imaginations of anthropologists, former or contemporary anthropophagists have multiplied with the advance of civilization and fieldwork in formerly unstudied culture areas. The existence of man-eating peoples just beyond the pale of civilization is a common ethnographic suggestion. When the Mediterranean was the center of the European cultural universe, Herodotus assumed that the custom flourished in Eastern Europe, while Strabo had the same fear about the barbarians on the western fringe. Thus, in good company and classic form, a recent encyclopedia of anthropology for today's generation of students reports that cannibalism "is practiced today only in the remotest parts of New Guinea and South America" (Koch 1976: 66). Like the poor, cannibals are always with us, but happily just beyond the possibility of actual observation.

The professional ethnographers do not actually state outright that they have observed the custom, nor do they condemn it. Instead, they are simply passing on these reports in what they deem to be a properly detached fashion. However, it would be naive not to recognize that this message will be interpreted in another fashion by the non-professional audience. The insistence on the cannibal theme has a number of consequences, which include a transformation of the scientific concepts into a more popular notion of savagery. This is neither surprising nor unexpected, for the shaping of public images of the mysterious corners of the world has always been a function of the traveler. This formerly haphazard arrangement has now become institutionalized as the discipline of anthropology in the industrialized societies. The process of providing the opportunity for the emergence of a professional class of students of the culturally unknown has created a more complex communication system. The needs and interests of those who create and select the information to be passed along must be considered as an additional factor.

As a consequence, the communication between specialist and layman has become a subtle one. In addition to collecting, translating and filtering the requisite data, anthropology has often served as a reviver and reinventor of the notion of savagery. The Aztecs again provide an example. In the sixteenth century, they were initially defined by the first generation of ethnographers as savages because of ritual cannibalism. In time this notion waned as for a long period their well-deserved cultural achievements were lauded. Today, the second generation of ethnographers restores the balance by refocusing our attention on cannibalism, which is now seen by some as having been more extensive than was ever imagined by these misguided friars who did not possess the scientific attitude and knowledge of their contemporary colleagues. Again it must be mentioned that the circumstantial evidence for Aztec cannibalism has not expanded by the recent discovery of unknown material on their traditional culture. Rather, the anthropologists now claim command over more sophisticated techniques for the measurement of demographic and caloric factors in the hope of solving the riddle of Aztec sacrifice. This means that, instead of simply adding to the literature, anthropology also provides a liberal and pseudo-scientific explanation for what our culture defines as savage behavior by instructing the laymen in the intricacies attending to the study of other cultures.

The anthropologist suggests that the natives in question were really not as barbaric as they might seem at first glance to the uninitiated reader. According to the specialists who seek the hidden, true meaning of "these barbarous practices" (Murdock 1934: 395), the people only ate tiny bits of human flesh during secret rituals or during mortuary services as a mark of respect for the deceased, or only resorted to this device on a larger scale due to a lack of adequate protein resources to support the population. Thus, anthropologists propose that the native behavior is comprehensible and even excusable when more esoteric scientific measures are brought to bear on the moral problem. In this way, they make a claim to be both subjective and scientific arbiters of the human condition.

This is an opportune moment to recall the great debates of the mid-sixteenth century between the major intellectual figures of the Spanish empire on the question of the moral propensities of the New World Indians. The controversy among contemporary academics as to whether the Aztecs ate human flesh in response to the demands of their religion or their environment is a direct descendant of this liberal trend in western scholarship. Against the charge that these cannibalistic Indians were the natural moral inferiors of the Spaniards, their defender Las Casas countered with the argument that they were merely misguided souls who could be saved by the Christian civilizing mission. Needless to say, Las Casas's flexible frame of mind was defended by the more liberal-minded professors at the leading Spanish universities (Keen 1971: 81). One of the few bright spots, if it can be called such, in the history of the cannibal complex mythology has been the willingness of the intellectuals of the eras to rush forward to defend and absolve the man-eaters of their deeds. In our age, instead of learned friars with their mastery of canon law and Aristotelian logic, we encounter learned professors referring to caloric tables and Lévi-Strauss's structuralism to explain away cannibalism. In their respective eras, both have taken upon themselves the responsibility of defending the savage mind and body without giving the matter of evidence even minimal consideration. As we shall see, Indians without souls to be saved or bizarre customs to be interpreted would be of little value to missionaries or anthropologists. When it comes to working the native preserves, representatives of both groups are often found taking the same position.

Once having made the proper excuses for the benighted natives' former moral transgressions, the anthropological fieldworker is also able to report, as we have so often seen, that contact with western civilization has immediately resulted in the demise of this custom which our culture views with such fascination and horror. Fortunately, but strangely enough, this is often the only trait which has been abandoned by the indigenes with such ease. Other customs which the agents of western morality also fail to appreciate, but which have actually been encountered, somehow manage to remain a vital part of the culture, in spite of determined efforts by others to stamp them out. A cynic might well suggest here that nothing disappears so easily as that which has never existed. Be that as it may, the modern ethnographer is justified in executing the mandate of his university and granting agency to report on exotic societies.

The typical apologetic reinterpretation of cannibalism may find an appreciative audience among other intellectuals, but it fails to dissuade the layman of the essential inferiority of those who are the subject of the discourse. Nor does the standard argument give the consumer reason to question the assumption of the moral and intellectual superiority of western civilization which is normally an intrinsic feature of the anthropological perspective. This attitude is typified by Margaret Mead, who so often served as a spokeswoman for American anthropology. Recently she was asked by a reporter for a popular magazine to account for her perennial optimism after so many years spent in the study of our species' often disheartening antics. Tellingly, she said: "But I have seen the children of head-hunters and cannibals becoming doctors and lawyers and dealing with complex mathematical and philosophical questions and walking around with *The Oxford Book of Verse*" (Anon. 1977: 25). From man-eaters to literary critics in one generation: what could be a finer testimonial to the gifts of western civilization? More than anything else, this sort of anthropological wisdom confirms already-existing value-laden notions about our own and other cultures by adding to them the props of liberalism and scientism. In sum, without the benefits of contemporary anthropology, the civilized world would be in danger of forgetting about extinct cannibals and would fail to be provided with new instances of live ones. Having kept the issue alive, anthropologists then nourish it in a hothouse of pseudo-intellectual science and misguided liberalism.

It is not difficult to see that our popular view of the cultural universe and its inhabitants is little different from the "we-they" dichotomy which prevails among the groups in other parts of the world which we hold as our intellectual inferiors. However, as befits a more complex society, we have the services of a distinct scholarly discipline to systematize the simple notions which must serve among primitive peoples. In ordering the material on other cultures, anthropology also serves as a medial category between us and them, represented by those who have lived in the two worlds and therefore claim to understand both the savage and the civilized mind. From this perspective, anthropologists emerge and function as classic middlemen in the ideological realm by serving two masters: one inhabits some corner of the world and provides the substance of their study; while the other fills the true center of their universe as the supporter and consumer of their cultural translations. At this intellectual juncture of two worlds, the anthropologist simultaneously generates and mediates differences through the explanation of cultural variation. In this way, points of contention are not completely resolved, for such a delicate position depends upon maintaining a requisite minimal degree of cultural tension and opposition. The process of providing a continuous justification for the idea that extant man-eaters still inhabit the farthest reaches of the globe, and then combating the cruder images this contention evokes by means of an often mystifying body of knowledge, is a well-fitting case in point.

In a collection of perceptive essays on the foundations and scope of social anthropology, one senior figure has remarked that the benefits of her thoughts were intended for the specialist and colleague, since anthropology has little influence over the way in which its contributions are interpreted and used by the public (Douglas 1975). This may be true to some extent, but it is also clear that in some instances the less erudite public does exactly what suits the scholars most in the sense of providing them with a continuing socially approved function. Therefore, if anthropologists were to undermine the symbolically charged cannibalistic boundary, the outcome would be fraught with potential danger. Merely entertaining the possibility of a universal taboo on cannibalism would affect the public's image and support of the discipline. The expected and so far successful task of the anthropologist has been to elucidate how we are both similar to and at the same time different from other human populations. Going to the extreme in either direction runs counter to meaningful and well-defined popular notions about human variability. The savages can be neither too noble nor too ignoble.

If this line of reasoning is correct, then anthropology has a clear-cut vested interest in maintaining some crucial cultural boundaries—of which the cannibalistic boundary is one—and constantly reinforcing subjective conclusions about the opposition between the civilized and savage. As an anthropologist, I do not find this an easy conclusion to arrive at or maintain. However, I am hard pressed to explain on other than these grounds the pervasiveness and tenacity of the belief in cannibalism based upon the flimsiest of often contradictory hearsay evidence. Many examples have already been called upon to support this contention, but another demonstrates a further facet of the problem.

A British officer traveling in northern Japan during the nineteenth century wrote that, although one missionary had reported on Ainu cannibalism, he himself was forced to voice his disagreement, which he made clear with the following comments:

From my own personal experience—and I may add I am the only foreigner who has seen these Tokachi . . . I came to a conclusion very different from this. I found that not only were they not cannibals, but that, taken altogether, they were the most peaceable, gentle and kind Ainu I came across during my peregrinations through the land of the hairy people. . . . I have no wish to force my opinion on the public as the correct one. I do but describe what I have actually seen in a district in which others who have written on the subject have never set foot, and I leave it to my readers to judge who has most claim to be heard [Landor 1893: 139].

The candid Landor would be justifiably disappointed to learn that in the twentieth century, among those who have made a profession of studying other cultures, the missionary assertion is more acceptable, since the Ainu are listed in the Human Relations Area Files under the culture trait "cannibalism." He would more than likely be horrified to find his name listed in the same place as a potential source for Ainu man-eating. This tendency of anthropologists to colorfully portray others as categorically different from ourselves is not unique to this problem, nor has it gone entirely unnoticed. Lévi-Strauss, the master of structuralism, has remarked that in his review of the literature on totemism he was led to an unexpected conclusion. He writes:

the comparison with totemism suggests a relation of another order between scientific theories and culture, one in which the mind of the scholar himself plays as large a part as the minds of the people studied; it is as though he were seeking, consciously or unconsciously, and under the guise of scientific objectivity, to make the latter—whether mental patients or so called "primitives"—more *different* than they really are [Lévi-Strauss 1963: 1; author's emphasis].

This profound insight did not prevent the author from elaborating elsewhere a classificatory system for cannibalism (Lévi-Strauss 1969), but his initial point remains valid.

Just prior to these additional comments on the problem of evidence, it was suggested that anthropologists were implicitly maintaining the cannibal notion for the sake of public interest and support. However, this is not the entire story, for no single explanation could adequately explicate the nature of this subtle intellectual complex. Lévi-Strauss's remarks on the nature of the scientific mind stimulate another line of reasoning which considers how both anthropologists and public define the proper perspective of the discipline and its practitioners. An idea which deserves much merit for elucidating some of the finer features of the problem was offered by a German colleague who was struggling in much the same manner as I with the topic of cannibalism (Frank 1977). Some background information which led to the communication between us permits a deeper understanding of the significance of his idea.

In carrying out library research on cannibalism for the sake of isolating some detailed reports which were absent in the more available publications, I was disturbed by the lack of documentation. Some time thereafter I presented some observations on this in a preliminary form to an audience of anthropologists who

THE MAN-EATING MYTH

reacted politely enough but advised checking additional sources. The recommendations were duly followed, but in addition I placed a notice in the *Newsletter* of the American Anthropological Association, soliciting those who had actually witnessed cannibalism, the act itself, to contact me. I assumed there must be some fieldworkers among the still-practicing cannibals of the interior of South America and New Guinea I often heard about who might be willing to share their first-hand experiences. I received four responses, but not of the type expected. One anthropologist referred me to a second, who said the first must be mistaken, but suggested a third, who answered that the second was confused, and the trail ended. It would be unrealistic to assume that there was some reticence about admitting to having observed the custom, since as it turned out it would have been an anthropological scoop. I then received a note from a philosopher, requesting I share my responses with him, since he was interested in the cessation of cannibalism as a significant stage in the moral development of other cultures. The third response came from New Guinea itself, and was penned by a psychiatrist, who wrote that, although he had not observed the deed, he had in his care a psychotic who claimed to have killed and eaten part of his son— for the sake of inducing the deity to deliver a cargo of western manufactured goods.

Finally, somewhat later, there arrived the fourth and most surprising response from a German graduate student who had chosen the analysis of cannibalism in the Amazon as his dissertation topic. He had run into one problem, though. His search of all the publications from the sixteenth to the twentieth century had failed to produce a single first-hand account of the act itself in this, one of the last preserves of man-eaters. Almost all of the books he read mentioned its existence, but as usual they were relying on other sources which never materialized as eyewitness accounts. He wondered if I could help him by sharing my responses from those of our colleagues who had indeed come into contact with practicing anthropophagists. I informed him none had come forward, and presented some of my conclusions. He admitted he had proposed some parallel ideas to his university examiners, who decided that, in light of their knowledge of the massive available evidence on cannibalism for this cultural area, he was mistaken. The fact that they had never looked at the documents, while he had examined them meticulously, did not seem to matter in the least. In addition to the charge of ignorance of the facts, his mentors also suggested that he was too enamored of these Indians who were the subject of his research to accept the idea that they would resort to the type of behavior western morality found repugnant. He was apparently reminded that these were South American Indians, not civilized Europeans. In other words, the senior scholars were accusing their student of ethnocentricism for his failure to accept their prejudicial views. With this situation in mind, especially in terms of the sanctions and rewards, it is now easier to appreciate how the Bangwa children mentioned earlier begin to accept their elders' view of cannibalistic sky witches among an illiterate people half a world away.

Frank's interpretation of this typical incident is telling. Often the response of colleagues to the idea that the cannibal notion is unsubstantiated provides a clue to the nature of the concept's meaning and function for the anthropologist. Frank suggests that the uncritical acceptance of cannibalism is a primary means by which anthropologists can convey their identification with the discipline's basic premise of cultural relativism, which admits to the existence of all possible variations of human behavior. The blasé and seemingly detached objective analysis of the purported practice also indicates a moral relativity which is a further hallmark of the professional mind. What others see as a social defect, the anthropologist finds to be nothing more than a curious custom or enigma which is as worthy of study as any other odd cultural trait. Thus to immediately accept and then fail to explicitly moralize on the cannibal nature of others is to be an anthropologist. The process illustrates the shedding of the ethnocentric mantle which is assumed to distinguish the lay public from the professional. This attitude also has a personal meaning, for often my insistence on reliable evidence to support the assumption of cannibalism has been interpreted by colleagues as repugnance or a refusal to admit the possibility of the practice. This is taken as an indication of an unscientific or ethnocentric turn of mind. As Frank has discovered, it is not easy to continue to pursue the problem in an objective fashion in the face of such delicate but nonetheless serious innuendoes. I do not mean to imply that anthropologists are engaged in a conscious intellectual conspiracy to delude the other members of their culture, or to arbitrarily enforce their collective views on individual doubters. Yet at the same time it must be recognized, as Lévi-Strauss has remarked, that the mind of the anthropologist is often at play in the fields of human nature. Reflections on the nature of the discipline, which very much involves a shared world-view, invite such a suspicion.

Anthropology's insistent dependence on the cannibal and on the aura of bemused scientific detachment is no more evident than in introductory textbooks which, on this issue, confirm and give systematic form to the prevailing notions of each generation. One such volume (Pearson 1974: 255) presents a picture of an African with filed incisor teeth; the author, in agreement with Arab slave traders, informs the student that such filing "is a frequent custom among cannibals." The individual in question is none other than a Zande, who, we have learned from those who were never among them, had ceased to be man-eaters a century earlier, when they were pacified by European colonial agents. In fact, what this particular author offers as evidence is the attitude of their northern neighbors, who have traditionally held the Azande and related peoples as their cultural inferiors (Buxton 1973). Another educational enterprise of this type (Collins 1973) chooses to illustrate an economic lesson on redistributive systems by describing how the parts of an enemy captive "are" allocated during a cannibalistic feast among the never-to-be-forgotten Tupinamba. The writer uses the present tense to relate the event, even though the case is taken from another anthropologist's essay composed some thirty years earlier (Métraux 1948), which relied upon Staden's sixteenth-century reminiscences. The fact that those being analyzed so dispassionately failed to survive the sixteenth century is not mentioned, and apparently this fact did not suggest to the author that it might be proper to shift to the past tense.

Then we have the case of an extremely popular text which mentions for no apparent reason, and with no citation, that prisoners in the Congo were penned and fattened for a feast "like the hand-stuffed geese of France" (Hoebel 1972: 147). Thus, the normal undergraduate enters the university with little idea about the study of man and the nebulous belief in cannibalism and departs some years later with a finer feel for the subtleties of both anthropophagy and anthropology. The undergraduate's parents, who might have missed the benefits of a higher education but are broadening their horizons through tourism to Hawaii, can be similarly informed at the gift shop of an important anthropological museum there. Here they can purchase "Authentic Cannibal Forks" made in Fiji which, the package instructs the buyer, were originally used by the chiefs, since it was *tapu* for such food to touch their "lips." It adds that missionaries stopped the practice, and suggests instead that the owner can now use these instruments as "pickle forks."

Undermining or reorienting popular misconceptions has always been a recognized function of the intellectual elite in any era. This is never an easy task, but nonetheless scholarly communities have achieved some laudable victories in their internal civilizing mission. Their contributions have also had moral overtones, since academic endeavors may very often encourage a more sophisticated ethical as well as intellectual view of the universe and its inhabitants. Consequently, intimating the possibility that scholarship can have the opposite function in some instances is particularly difficult. Taking issue with the revered notions of the scientist is an onerous affair because the gifted and educated, rather than the less sophisticated congregation, are the most intransigent in the face of assaults on what are commonly assumed to be self-evident truths. The laity in any context is accustomed to being instructed. However, those who have become comfortable with the complementary responsibility of enlightening naturally enough take a dim view of having to question their basic premises. Novel ideas about previously unconsidered problems are encouraged and applauded, as befits the intellectual life-style; and it must be admitted that these achievements bring credit and legitimacy to a group often viewed with some suspicion. Radical reinterpretations of long-standing issues are another matter, for they indirectly cast doubt on the value and performance of those who have claimed social support in return for their devotion to the expansion of knowledge.

In effect, in particular instances, the intellectual mandarins have a greater stake in maintaining the scholarly *status quo* than those engaged in more practical affairs, who are as willing to accept on faith new facts or the reinterpretation of what was once assumed to be known. The subtle difference between the two types of advances have meaning only for those who are most seriously affected. To accept the idea that those most intimately involved in the world of ideas have an undiluted, unqualified commitment to the truth, wherever this may lead them, is to miss the message of some of the more profound lessons of western scholarship. When it comes to a confrontation between science and cosmology, it would be overly idealistic to conclude that the former always triumphs over the latter, even among the intelligentsia.

Illustrations of the clash between such ideals and ideas are not rare in the history of western thought. Scenes of the struggle between traditional healer and physician, alchemist and chemist, astrologer and astronomer, are easily evoked, but not entirely satisfactory, analogies. These instances distort the image, for they involve the competition between radically divergent systems of thought, rather than a peculiar blind spot in what is an otherwise coherent and established contemporary view of human nature.

An example with closer resemblances to the complex cast of figures who play out their preordained roles in the cannibal drama of this era is again provided by a comparison with a sixteenth-century social phenomenon. Historians often help us see the present more clearly than those disciplines which make a greater claim to the privilege.

The incident in question is of course the European witch-craze referred to earlier, portrayed and analyzed by Trevor-Roper. He points out that, in the era we now refer to as the Dark Ages, there may have been a vague folklore about witches, but no systemized demonology. This mythology was not constructed and put to its terrible use until the sixteenth century. Most interesting is his assertion that this "rubbish of the human mind" (1969: 97), which resulted in the annihilation of untold thousands—for, among other things, lying with the devil, murdering infants for their flesh and fat, mounting airborne broomsticks and flying goats—was the concoction of the urbane and civilized mind. The scattered ideas of the ignorant were organized into a coherent view of the supernatural and made fashionable by Renaissance Popes, Protestant reformers, saints of the Counter-Reformation and a host of other secular and sacred scholars. These intellectual fantasies, which he compares to the psychopathic delusions of the madhouse, were beyond the imagination of the peasantry but came easily to the more fertile intellects of the age. Trevor-Roper cautions that it would be mistaken to lay all of this at the feet of mere academic hacks alone, for some of the great minds, still acknowledged today for their intellectual grace, turned to the study of witches and demons with unflinching vigor. Their more abstract and esoteric formulations were then given substance by the minor functionaries in the field, who never failed to encounter suspicious circumstantial manifestations of this evil among the local populace in the recesses of the European continent. Even less responsible were the laymen, who were unable to grasp the more learned details and discussions supplied by the experts. These ruminations could only be interpreted, not without resistance and difficulty, in a vague way by the masses as a more learned confirmation of their own less developed preconceptions.

Those scholars whom Trevor-Roper refers to as having taken refuge in "the scepticism of common sense," due to their inability to accept the possibility of flying broomsticks, the devil incarnate and the admissions of the tortured and ignorant, placed themselves in some peril. These skeptics were denounced by the defenders of the orthodox vision as being ignorant, spiritually lax and potentially in league with the devil and his helpers on earth. This elaborate myth, which was given credence in almost all quarters, eventually collapsed and retreated to the realm of superstition from which it had emerged. Yet the doctrine ruled the minds of men, including the most enlightened, for two centuries before its ultimate demise. Lacking the usual hallmarks of responsible scholarship and civil administration which both preceded and followed the witch-craze era, this period of intellectual aberration, Trevor-Roper suggests, can only be understood in terms of the general tenor of the times and more specifically in light of the way in which the mythology served the particular interests of clerics, academics, jurists and temporal rulers.

This chronological detour was not resorted to in the belief that it offers exact parallels to the contemporary cosmos of cannibals and their interpreters, nor was it designed to create unnecessarily disparaging comparisons. However, momentarily confining the focus to the sixteenth and seventeenth centuries permits some legitimate, instructive analogies to be drawn, making it possible to show how similar cultural themes gave rise to related images of European witchcraft and New World cannibalism. For reasons which can no longer be fully comprehended, the collective mind of that era was beset by Christian heretics, alien Jews and American Indians who committed unspeakable crimes involving the use of human flesh and blood. That these notions were based on unreliable evidence and flew in the face of common sense and decency was of no account. Those Dominican friars who took pride in their title and function as "the hounds of God" roamed the world in search of their inevitable finds. They may now have to accept a major share of the responsibility for the misguided efforts of an age, but at the time their views were embraced by all.

Shifting now to a comparison of this era with our own, and leaving ethical considerations aside, we find various resemblances. First, it is not too difficult to appreciate that a certain notion, whether of cannibalism or witchcraft, can be sustained by layman and intellectual alike, with the latter taking the lead in converting vulgar suppositions into more elegant scientific dogma. Second, there is the correlation between the ways in which the eventual conclusions have been employed to serve the interests of the specialized group which has propounded them in the form of intellectual excesses. Finally, there is the lesson to be drawn which attests to the fact of there always being the possibility, no matter how remote, that conventional and scientific wisdom may be erroneous views of the universe.

In addition to requiring a brief suspension of some preexisting notions, this book has asked the reader to brave the onslaught of myriad ethnographic facts, contrasting theoretical schools of thought, widely separated historical periods, and finally the labyrinth of the human mind expressing itself in various times and places. This test of the intellect was necessitated by the nature of the cannibal complex, but it is also what makes the problem such an intriguing one. The argument has also had to take a number of twists and turns in order to stay close to the material, thus creating the possibility of misinterpretation; so I shall restate here some of the points made earlier, as well as those which were not intended to be drawn.

With regard to the second category, which in some ways is the most important, I have stated my reservations on the matter, but nonetheless have consciously avoided suggesting that customary cannibalism in some form does not or has never existed.

THE MAN-EATING MYTH

This is not intellectual vacillation, but rather derives from an appreciation of the problem and from methodological rigor. The only proper theoretical stance for an anthropologist to take demands an open mind on the possibility of cultural variation, and this would include cannibalism. According to standard ethnographic methodology, it is not possible to demonstrate conclusively that a practice does not exist. Reporting the custom to be unobserved or undocumented is the best one can hope to do. Moreover, it is more reasonable for those who would claim a certain activity is prevalent to bear the major burden of proof. It follows, therefore, that it has not been possible to demonstrate that cannibalism did not take place among the Caribs, Aztecs, West Africans and the Fore, who were examined in some detail. At the same time, and this provides a more meaningful insight into the problem, it has been equally difficult to show that the very same custom did not prevail among Christians, Jews and medieval heretics. For these groups the common assertion that maybe they did practice cannibalism but then immediately ceased upon being told to do so or thereafter hid it from the authorities no longer seems so credible. Even if the custom did prevail among some of the former groups, this would still fail to account adequately for the ubiquitous tendency to label others as cannibals. That world-view is a different issue only tenuously related to the question of whether or not the Aztecs or Fore were really man-eaters.

Turning now to the more positive contribution of this survey, I have stated that despite an extensive review of highly recommended and generally accepted basic sources, it was not possible to isolate a single reliable complete first-hand account by an anthropologist of this purported conventional way of disposing of the dead. The legion of existing reports by non-specialists were found to range from highly suspect to entirely groundless when viewed from the perspective of objective scholarship and common sense. Those members of the anthropological fraternity who would readily admit that the custom has been blown out of proportion to its actual occurrence by the laity are merely retreating behind the transparent claim of possessing arcane knowledge not available to the uninitiated. However, this assertion is nothing more than an academic ideological strategy based upon similarly vague preconceptions lacking a solid historical or ethnographic foundation.

These considerations have led to the conclusion that, although the theoretical possibility of customary cannibalism cannot be dismissed, the available evidence does not permit the facile assumption that the act was or has ever been a prevalent cultural feature. It is more reasonable to conclude that the idea of the cannibalistic nature of others is a myth in the sense of, first, having an independent existence bearing no relationship to historical reality, and second, containing and transmitting significant cultural messages for those who maintain it. At the concrete level of experience, this means that the idea precedes whatever evidence has been offered to support it and that in some instances the position is maintained in spite of evidence to the contrary. At a more profound level the story line instructs us, as well as those of other cultures, on the basic nature of savage and civilized behavior. Therefore, I have suggested that the more intriguing question is concerned with anthropophagy and anthropology as interdependent views of the world. Both can be interpreted as closed systems of thought, failing to recognize the obvious inconsistencies and contradictions which are themselves meaningful facets of the mental construct.

The explanations offered to account for the belief in cannibalism, including those derived from willing informants, were obvious and simple ones—if not basic themes and techniques of social anthropology when other topics are under discussion. The misguided notions about the savage mode of life have fallen, one by one, against its onslaught, but the cannibal remains inviolate, never to be seen or forgotten. In a sense, social anthropologists of all persuasions have had to avoid applying their own lessons to the study of their own discipline for the purpose of maintaining a crude cultural opposition between "we" and "they." As a consequence, the general tone of modern anthropological commentary on cannibalism emerges as little more than nineteenth-century reinterpretations in contemporary scientific jargon. In the process, those claiming to possess the anthropological imagination have failed to bring to bear the modern insights which have deepened our appreciation of related cultural patterns. Admittedly, our information on other cultures has expanded greatly over the past hundred years. However, there is a subtle but crucial difference between knowledge and understanding which this review of the cannibal literature attests to. Instead of seeking a less obvious but more profound meaning for informants' statements on the cannibals in the mythological past, presently among them or in an adjacent territory, anthropologists have assumed an attitude defined by one practitioner who is not a westerner by birth as "vicarious ethnocentricism." In the neighboring cannibals instance, this position involved the adoption of one foreign culture's negative evaluation of another. This permits in good conscience the legitimate expression of corresponding western biases in the guise of objective ethnography (Legesse 1973: 276–78). Understandably, the subjective ruses scholars have the opportunity to resort to are more subtle than those normally encountered in the pedestrian literature which they take delight in debunking with regularity.

This inquiry has not always been totally dispassionate in tone, but specific moral and ethical issues have been purposely left aside in order to focus on other issues. However, this is the moment to propose that if our discipline has any ethical responsibility on this matter, it demands that we put our house in order by objectively reassessing some oppressive mental constructs rather than solicitously concerning ourselves with giving more coherent form to public misconceptions. Beyond that, anthropology has no special moral obligation except the scholarly injunction to seek the truth regardless of the implications this may have for the discipline. This is no small matter, for as we have seen, when the intellectual elite have lent their weight to a moral crusade, western civilization has made some of its poorest showings in historical annals. I do not mean to imply that intellectuals must bear a major responsibility for the political excesses of the societies they serve. Among other considerations, this would be a form of collective egomania, for scholars have never enjoyed the actual power the idea presupposes. Nor does the anthropological contribution to the cannibal complex rival in depth or scope some other scientific perversions which have accompanied some truly barbaric twentieth-century outbursts. Yet it is not possible to divorce entirely the way in which the cannibal notion has been manipulated by scholar and layman alike from its use as ideological justification for some very real forms of human exploitation.

Enough has been said on this matter, for my purpose here has not been entirely negative. For this reason, in recognition of the fact that a prevailing assumption of social anthropology lacks the theoretical sophistication and scholarly foundation normally demanded, I have sought on the positive side to explain this situation rather than merely denouncing it. This avenue of inquiry has led to the conclusion that our culture, like many others, finds comfort in the idea of the barbarian just beyond the gates. What is unique is that our type of society gives succor to specialized interpreters of this exotic image whose function condemns them to a never-ending search for the primitive in order to give meaning to the concept of civilization (cf. Diamond 1976). This discipline also depends in part on the existence of the savage, hence the cannibal. Without anthropophagists, anthropologists would find themselves in much the same position as the inquisitors of the Middle Ages, who quickly exhausted the supply of mortal heretics and therefore had to conjure up supernatural ones lest their industry and wisdom become superfluous. The following quote by the historian Cohn makes many of these points more elegantly than these pages have been able to do. Thus it serves as an apt conclusion:

Now the notion of a flying sect of heretics had great advantages: it made it possible to account for assemblies which were frequent and often vast, and which nevertheless nobody ever saw [1975: 228].

If Cohn's message is correct, and it is difficult to imagine otherwise, then this dissertation will fail to alter immediately our contemporary picturesque representation of evil, but it may serve as a beginning.

BIBLIOGRAPHY

Aguilar, Francisco de. 1963. "The Chronicle of Fray Francisco de Aguilar." In *The Conquistadors*, ed. Patricia de Fuentes, pp. 134–64. New York: The Orion Press.

Alldridge, T. J. 1901. *The Sherbro and Its Hinterland*. London: Macmillan and Co.

Alpers, M. P. 1966. "Epidemiological Changes in Kuru." In *Slow, Latent and Temperate Virus Infections*, ed. D. C. Gajdusek, pp. 65–82. Washington, D.C.: HEW.

———. 1970. "Kuru: Changing Patterns." *American Journal of Tropical Medicine and Hygiene* 19:133–37.

———, et al. 1975. *Bibliography of Kuru*. 3rd ed. Bethesda: National Institutes of Health.

Alvarado, Pedro de. 1963. "Two Letters of Pedro de Alvarado." In *The Conquistadors*, ed. Patricia de Fuentes, pp. 182–96. New York: The Orion Press.

Anon. 1977. "The Talk of the Town." *The New Yorker*, 3 March, p. 23.

Anonymous Conquistador. 1963. "The Chronicle of the Anonymous Conquistador." In *The Conquistadors*, ed. Patricia de Fuentes, pp. 165–81. New York: The Orion Press.

Ardrey, Robert. 1976. *The Hunting Hypothesis*. New York: Atheneum.

Bandelier, Fanny R. 1971. "Fray Bernardino de Sahagún." In *A History of Ancient Mexico*, by Fray Bernardino de Sahagún. Detroit: Blaine Ethridge Books.

Barth, Fredrik. 1975. *Ritual and Knowledge among the Baktaman of New Guinea*. New Haven: Yale University Press.

Beatty, K. J. 1915. *Human Leopards*. London: Hugh Rees.

Bergounioux, F. M. 1961. "Notes on the Mentality of Primitive Man." In *Social Life of Early Man*, ed. S. L. Washburn, pp. 106–18. Chicago: Aldine Publishing Co.

Berndt, R. M. 1952. "A Cargo Movement in the Eastern Central Highlands of New Guinea." *Oceania* 23:40-65; 23:137-58.

———. 1954. "Reaction to Contact in the Eastern Highlands of New Guinea." *Oceania* 24:190-228; 24:255-74.

———. 1958. "A Devastating Disease Syndrome: Kuru Sorcery in the Eastern Highlands of New Guinea." *Sociologus* 8:4-28.

———. 1962. *Excess and Restraint.* Chicago: University of Chicago Press.

Berry, R. G. 1912. "The Sierra Leone Cannibals, with Notes on their History, Religion and Customs." *Proceedings of the Royal Irish Academy* 30:15-69.

Blanc, Alberto. 1961. "Some Evidence for the Ideologies of Early Man." In *Social Life of Early Man*, ed. S. L. Washburn, pp. 119-36. Chicago: Aldine Publishing Co.

Brain, Robert. 1970. "Child Witches." In *Witchcraft, Accusations and Confessions*, ed. Mary Douglas, pp. 161-79. London: Tavistock Publications.

Breuil, H., and Lantier, R. 1965. *The Men of the Old Stone Age,* trans. B. B. Rafter. New York: St. Martin's Press.

Brooks, Van Wyck. 1924. Introduction to *Journal of the First Voyage to America*, by Christopher Columbus. New York: Albert & Charles Boni.

Brothwell, D. R. 1961. "Cannibalism in Early Britain." *Antiquity* 35:304-7.

Burnet, F. M. 1971. "Reflections on Kuru." *Human Biology in Oceania* 1:3-9.

Buxton, Jean. 1973. *Religion and Healing in Mandari.* Oxford: The Clarendon Press.

Cerwin, Herbert. 1963. *Bernal Díaz.* Norman: University of Oklahoma Press.

Clerk, Christian. 1975. "The Cannibal Sign." *RAIN* 8:1-3.

Cohn, Norman. 1975. *Europe's Inner Demons.* London: Chatto Heinemann for Sussex University.

Collins, John J. 1975. *Anthropology: Culture, Society and Evolution.* Englewood Cliffs, N.J.: Prentice-Hall.

Columbus, Christopher. 1968. *The Journal of Christopher Columbus*, trans. Cecil Jane. London: Anthony Blond.

Coon, Carleton C. 1963. *The Origin of Races*. New York: Alfred A. Knopf.

Cortés, Hernando. 1962. *Five Letters 1519-1526*, trans. J. B. Morris. New York: W. W. Norton & Co.

———. 1963. "The Third Letter of Hernan Cortés." In *The Conquistadors*, ed. Patricia de Fuentes, pp. 49-133. New York: The Orion Press.

Crocombe, R. G., and Crocombe, Marjorie. 1968. *The Works of Ta'unga*. Honolulu: University of Hawaii Press.

d'Anghera, Peter Martyr. 1912. *De Orbe Novo*, trans. F. A. Mac Nutt. 2 vols. New York: G. P. Putnam's Sons.

Dart, Raymond A. 1953. "The Predatory Transition from Ape to Man." *International Anthropological and Linguistic Review* 1:201-13.

de Mortillet, G. 1886. "Anthropophagie (Paléoethnologie)." In *Dictionnaire des Sciences Anthropologiques*. Vol. 1. Paris: Marpon et Flammarion.

Diamond, Stanley. 1976. *In Search of the Primitive*. New Brunswick, N.J.: Transaction Books.

Díaz del Castillo, Bernal. 1970. *The Discovery and Conquest of Mexico*, trans. Irving A. Leonard. New York: Octagon Books.

Dole, Gertrude. 1962. "Endocannibalism among the Amahuaca Indians." *Transactions of the New York Academy of Science* (Series II) 24:567-73.

D'Olwer, Luis N., and Cline, Howard F. 1973. "Sahagún and His Works." In *Handbook of Middle American Indians*, ed. Howard F. Cline, Vol. 13: *Guide to Ethnohistorical Sources*, pp. 186-89. Austin: University of Texas Press.

Dornstreich, M. D., and Morren, G. E. B. 1974. "Does New Guinea Cannibalism Have Nutritional Value?" *Human Ecology* 2:1-12.

Douglas, Mary. 1970. *Natural Symbols*. London: Barrie and Rockliff.

———. 1975. *Implicit Meanings*. London: Routledge & Kegan Paul.

Durán, Fray Diego. 1964. *The Aztecs: The History of the Indies of New Spain*, trans. and eds. D. Heyden and F. Horcasitas. New York: Orion Press.

————. 1971. *Book of the Gods and Rites and the Ancient Calendar*, trans. and eds. F. Horcasitas and D. Heyden. Norman: University of Oklahoma Press.

Eames, Wilberforce. 1922. "Description of a Wood Engraving Illustrating the South American Indians (1505)." *Bulletin of the New York Public Library* 26:755–60.

Evans-Pritchard, E. E. 1956. "Cannibalism: A Zande Text." *Africa* 26:73–74.

————. 1965. "Zande Cannibalism." In *The Position of Women in Primitive Societies and Other Essays in Social Anthropology*, pp. 133–64. London: Faber and Faber.

Fallers, Lloyd A. 1969. *Law Without Precedent*. Chicago: University of Chicago Press.

Fischer, Ann, and Fischer, J. L. 1960. "Aetiology of Kuru." *The Lancet* 1:1417–18.

————. 1961. "Culture and Epidemiology." *Journal of Health and Human Behavior* 2:16–25.

————. 1962. "An Anthropological View of Kuru." Presented at the Nineteenth Annual Meeting of the American Public Health Association, Miami Beach. Mimeo.

Fischer, J. L., et al. 1976. "Ponopean Concepts of Incest." *The Journal of the Polynesian Society* 85:199–207.

Flinn, Lynn, et al. 1976. "Additional Evidence for Cannibalism in the Southwest: The Case of LA 4528." *American Antiquity* 41:308–18.

Frank, Erwin. 1977. Personal communication.

Freeman, Derek. 1964. "Human Aggression in an Anthropological Perspective." In *The Natural History of Aggression*, eds. J. D. Carthy and F. J. Ebling, pp. 109–19. London: Academic Press.

Freud, Sigmund. 1950. *Totem and Taboo*. New York: W. W. Norton & Co.

Fyfe, Christopher. 1962. *A History of Sierra Leone*. London: Oxford University Press.

Gajdusek, D. C. 1963. "Kuru." *Transactions of the Royal Society of Tropical Medicine and Hygiene* 57:151–69.

———. 1965. "Kuru in New Guinea and the Origin of the NINDB Study of Slow, Latent, and Temperate Virus Infections of the Nervous System of Man." In *Slow, Latent, and Temperate Virus Infections*, eds. D. C. Gajdusek, et al., pp. 3–12. Washington, D. C.: HEW.

———. 1970. Introduction to "Isolated and Migratory Population Groups." *American Journal of Tropical Medicine and Hygiene* 19:127–29.

———. 1976. *Correspondence on the Discovery and Original Investigations on Kuru*. Bethesda: National Institutes of Health.

———, and Zigas, V. 1957. "Degenerative Disease of the Central Nervous System in New Guinea." *New England Journal of Medicine* 257:974–78.

———. 1961. "The Ethnographic Setting of Kuru." *The American Journal of Tropical Medicine and Hygiene* 10:80–91.

———. 1977. "Unconventional Viruses and the Origin and Disappearance of Kuru." *Science* 197:943–60.

———. 1978. Personal Communication.

———, et al. 1966. "Experimental Transmission of a *Kuru*-like Syndrome to Chimpanzees." *Nature* 204:257–59.

Garn, S. M., and Block, W. D. 1970. "The Limited Nutritional Value of Cannibalism." *American Anthropologist* 72:106.

George, Katherine. 1968. "The Civilized West Looks at Primitive Africa 1400–1800: A Study in Ethnocentrism." In *The Concept of the Primitive*, ed. Ashley Montagu, pp. 175–93. New York: The Free Press.

Gibbon, Edward. 1900. *The Decline and Fall of the Roman Empire*. Vol. 2. New York: Peter Fenelon Collier & Son.

Gibbs, C. J., and Gajdusek, D. C. 1974. "Biology of Kuru and Creutzfeld-Jakob Disease." In *Slow Virus Diseases*, eds. W. Zerman and E. H. Lennette, pp. 39–48. Baltimore: The Williams and Wilkens Co.

Gibson, Charles. 1964. *The Aztecs Under Spanish Rule*. Stanford: Stanford University Press.

Glasse, R. 1962. "The Spread of Kuru among the Fore." Department of Public Health, Territory of Papua New Guinea. Mimeo.

———. 1963. "Cannibalism in the Kuru Region." Department of Public Health, Territory of Papua and New Guinea. Mimeo.

———. 1967. "Cannibalism in the Kuru Region of New Guinea." *Transactions of the New York Academy of Sciences* 29:748–54.

———. 1970. "Some Recent Observations on Kuru." *Oceania* 40:210–13.

———, and Lindenbaum, S. 1976. "Kuru at Wanitabe." In *Essays on Kuru*, ed. R. W. Hornabrook, pp. 28–37. Faringdon, Berks.: E. W. Classey.

de Gómara, Francisco Lopez. 1964. *Cortés: The Life of the Conqueror by His Secretary*, trans. and ed. L. B. Simpson. Berkeley: University of California Press.

Goody, Jack. 1962. *Death, Property and the Ancestors*. Stanford: Stanford University Press.

Gossen, Gary H. 1975. "Animal Souls and Human Destiny in Chamula." *Man* (N.S.) 10:448–61.

Hallpike, C. R. 1977. *Bloodshed and Vengeance in the Papuan Mountains*. Oxford: The Clarendon Press.

Hanke, Lewis. 1974. *All Mankind Is One*. DeKalb: Northern Illinois University Press.

Harner, Michael. 1977a. "The Ecological Basis for Aztec Sacrifice." *American Ethnologist* 4:117–35.

———. 1977b. "The Enigma of Aztec Sacrifice." *Natural History* 76:47–51.

Harrell-Bond, B. E. 1975. "Patterns of Consumption." *The Times Literary Supplement*, October 17, pp. 1228–29.

Harris, Marvin. 1977. *Cannibals and Kings*. New York: Random House.

Hartman, Dean. 1975. "Preliminary Assessment of Mass Burials in the Southwest." *American Journal of Physical Anthropology* 42:305–6.

Helmuth, Herman. 1973. "Cannibalism in Paleoanthropology and Ethnology." In *Man and Aggression*, ed. Ashley Montagu, pp. 229–53. New York: Oxford University Press.

Herodotus. 1879. *A New and Literal Version*, trans. Henry Cary. London: George Bell & Sons.

Hinde, Sidney L. 1897. *The Fall of the Congo Arabs*. New York: Thomas Whittaker.

Hoebel, E. A. 1972. *Anthropology: The Study of Man*. New York: McGraw-Hill Book Co.

Hogg, Garry. 1973. *Cannibalism and Human Sacrifice*. London: Pan Books.

Hornabrook, R. W. 1975. "Kuru." In *Topics on Tropical Neurology*, ed. R. W. Hornabrook, pp. 71–90. Philadelphia: F. A. Davis.

———, and Moir, D. 1970. "Kuru: Epidemiological Trends." *The Lancet* 2:1175–79.

Huxley, Francis. 1957. *Affable Savages*. New York: The Viking Press.

Huxley, Thomas H. 1898. *Man's Place in Nature*. New York: D. Appleton and Co.

Jacob, T. 1972. "The Problem of Head-Hunting and Brain-Eating among Pleistocene Men in Indonesia." *Archaeology and Physical Anthropology in Oceania* 7:81–91.

Jenkins, Claude. 1968. "Christian Pilgrimages, A.D. 500–800." In *Travel and Travellers of the Middle Ages*, ed. A. P. Newton, pp. 39–69. New York: Barnes & Noble.

Johnston, H. 1902. *The Uganda Protectorate*. London: Hutchinson and Co.

Joset, Paul-Ernest. 1955. *Les Sociétiés secrètes des hommes-léopards en afrique noire*. Paris: Payot.

Kalous, Milan. 1974. *Cannibals and Tongo Players of Sierra Leone*. Auckland: Distributed by Kegan Paul, Trench, Trubner.

Keen, Benjamin. 1971. *The Aztec Image in Western Thought*. New Brunswick, N.J.: Rutgers University Press.

Kisch, Guido. 1949. *The Jews in Medieval Germany*. Chicago: University of Chicago Press.

Knivet, Anthonie. 1906. "The Admirable Adventures and Strange Fortunes of Master Anthonie Knivet." In *Hakluytus Posthumus or Purchas His Pilgrimes*, ed. Samuel Purchas. Vol. 16, pp. 177–289. Glasgow: James MacLehose and Sons.

Koch, Klaus-Friedrich. 1970a. "Cannibalistic Revenge in Jalé Warfare." *Natural History* 79:41–50.

———. 1970b. "Warfare and Anthropophagy in Jalé Society." *Bijdragen Tot De Taal-, Land-Em Volkenkunde* 126:37–55.

———. 1974. *War and Peace in Jalémó*. Cambridge, Mass.: Harvard University Press.

———. 1976. "Cannibalism." In *Encyclopedia of Anthropology*, eds. D. E. Hunter and P. Whitten, p. 66. New York: Harper & Row.

Labley, David. 1976. "Incest as Cannibalism: The Yapese Analysis." *The Journal of the Polynesian Society* 85:171–79.

Landor, A. H. S. 1893. *Alone with the Hairy Ainu*. London: John Murray.

Landtman, G. 1917. *The Folk Tales of the Kiwai Papuans*. Helsingfors, Sweden: Acta Societatis Scientiarum Fennicae.

———. 1927. *The Kiwai Papuans of British New Guinea*. London: Macmillan and Co.

Las Casas, Bartolomé de. 1971. *History of the Indies*, trans. Andrée Collard. New York: Harper & Row.

———. 1974. *In Defense of the Indians*, trans. Stafford Poole. DeKalb: Northern Illinois University Press.

Leakey, R., and Lewin, R. 1977. *Origins*. New York: E. P. Dutton.

Legesse, Asmarom. 1973. *Gada*. New York: The Free Press.

Leonard, Irving A. 1970. Translator's Commentary on *The Discovery and Conquest of Mexico*, by Bernal Díaz del Castillo. New York: Octagon Books.

Leon-Portilla, Miguel. 1962. *The Broken Spears*. London: Constable and Co.

Léry, Jean de. 1780. *Histoire d'un voyage faict en la terre du Brésil*. Vol. 2. Paris: Alphonse Lemerre.

Lévi-Strauss, Claude. 1963. *Totemism*, trans. Rodney Needham. Boston: Beacon Press.

———. 1966. "The Culinary Triangle." *Partisan Review* 33:586–95.

———. 1969. *The Raw and the Cooked*, trans. John and Doreen Weightman. New York: Harper and Row.

———. 1975. "Anthropologie Sociale." *Extrait de L'Annuaire du Collège de France, Resumé des Cours de 1974–1975* 75:347–53.

Levy, Robert I. 1973. *Tahitians*. Chicago: University of Chicago Press.

Lindenbaum, S. 1976. "A Wife Is the Hand of Man." In *Man and Woman in the New Guinea Highlands*, eds. Paula Brown and Georgeda Buchbinder, pp. 54-62. Washington, D.C.: American Anthropological Association.

Lindskog, Birger. 1954. *African Leopard Men*. Uppsala: The Swedish Research Council for Social Sciences.

Little, Kenneth. 1967. *The Mende of Sierra Leone*. London: Routledge & Kegan Paul.

Livingstone, David. 1874. *The Last Journals of David Livingstone in Central Africa, from 1865 to His Death*, ed. Horace Waller. Vol. 2. London: John Murray.

Lockhart, John Ingram. 1844. Translator's Preface to *The Discovery and Conquest of Mexico and New Spain*, by Bernal Díaz del Castillo. London: J. Hatchard and Son.

Loeb, E. M. 1964. *The Blood Sacrifice Complex*. New York: Kraus Reprint Corp.

Malefijt, A. 1968. "Homo Monstrosus." *Scientific American* 219:112-18.

Markham, Clements R. 1964. *Expeditions into the Valley of the Amazons*. New York: Burt Franklain.

Marsh, Richard. 1976. "The 1976 Nobel Prize for Physiology or Medicine." *Science* 194:928-29.

Marx, Karl, and Engels, Frederick. 1971. *Ireland and the Irish Question*. Moscow: Progress Publishers.

Mead, Margaret. 1950. *Sex and Temperament in Three Primitive Societies*. New York: Mentor Books.

Métraux, A. 1948. "The Tupi Namba." In *Handbook of South American Indians*, ed. Julian Steward. Vol. 3. New York: Cooper Square Press.

Middleton, John. 1970. *The Study of the Lugbara*. New York: Holt, Rinehart and Winston.

Miller, Joseph C. 1976. *Kings and Kinsmen*. Oxford: Clarendon Press.

Montagu, Ashley. 1937. "A Brief Excursion into Cannibalism." *Science* 86:56-57.

———. 1968. "The Fallacy of the Primitive." in *The Concept of the Primitive*, ed. Ashley Montagu, pp. 1–6. New York: The Free Press.

———. 1976. *The Nature of Human Aggression*. New York: Oxford University Press.

Montaigne, Michael de. 1952. "Of Cannibals." In *The Essays of Michael Eyquem Montaigne*, trans. and ed. Charles Colton. Chicago: Encyclopaedia Britannica.

Montellano, Bernard R. Ortiz de. 1978. "Aztec Cannibalism: An Ecological Necessity?" *Science* 200:611–17.

Murdock, George Peter. 1934. *Our Primitive Contemporaries*. New York: The Macmillan Co.

Murray, Margaret A. 1970. *The God of the Witches*. New York: Oxford University Press.

Needham, Rodney. 1972. *Belief, Language, and Experience*. Chicago: The University of Chicago Press.

———. 1973. "Prospects and Impediments." *The Times Literary Supplement*, July 6, pp. 785–86.

Newson, Linda A. 1976. *Aboriginal and Spanish Colonial Trinidad*. New York: Academic Press.

Parrinder, Geoffrey. 1963. *Witchcraft: European and African*. London: Faber and Faber.

Pearson, R. 1974. *Introduction to Anthropology*. New York: Holt, Rinehart and Winston.

Prescott, W. H. 1909. *The Conquest of Mexico*. 2 vol. London: J. M. Dent & Sons.

Price, Barbara J. 1978. "Demystification, Enriddlement, and Aztec Cannibalism: A Materialist Rejoinder to Harner." *American Ethnologist* 5:98–115.

Rappaport, Roy. 1968. *Pigs for the Ancestors*. New Haven: Yale University Press.

Rouse, Irving. 1948. "The Carib." In *Handbook of South American Indians*, ed. Julian Steward. Vol. 4, pp. 547–65. New York: Cooper Square Press.

———. 1964. "Prehistory of the West Indies." *Science* 144:499–513.

Sagan, Eli. 1974. *Cannibalism.* New York: Harper & Row.

Sahagún, Fray Bernardo de. 1950. *Florentine Codex: General History of the Things of New Spain.* Book 1: *The Gods,* trans. C. E. Dibble and A. J. O. Anderson. Santa Fe: The School of American Research.

————. 1951. *Florentine Codex: General History of the Things of New Spain.* Book 2: *The Ceremonies,* trans. C. E. Dibble and A. J. O. Anderson. Santa Fe: The School of American Research.

————. 1952. *Florentine Codex: General History of the Things of New Spain.* Book 3: *The Origin of the Gods,* trans. C. E. Dibble and A. J. O. Anderson. Santa Fe: The School of American Research.

————. 1953. *Florentine Codex: General History of the Things of New Spain.* Book 7: *The Sun, Moon, and Stars and the Binding of the Years,* trans. C. E. Dibble and A. J. O. Anderson. Santa Fe: The School of American Research.

————. 1955. *Florentine Codex: General History of the Things of New Spain.* Book 12: *The Conquest of Mexico,* trans. C. E. Dibble and A. J. O. Anderson. Santa Fe: The School of American Research.

————. 1957. *Florentine Codex: General History of the Things of New Spain.* Book 4: *The Soothsayers,* and Book 5: *The Omens,* trans. C. E. Dibble and A. J. O. Anderson. Santa Fe: The School of American Research.

————. 1958. *Florentine Codex: General History of the Things of New Spain.* Book 8: *Kings and Lords,* trans. C. E. Dibble and A. J. O. Anderson. Santa Fe: The School of American Research.

————. 1959. *Florentine Codex: General History of the Things of New Spain.* Book 9: *The Merchants,* trans. C. E. Dibble and A. J. O. Anderson. Santa Fe: The School of American Research.

Sauer, Carl O. 1966. *The Early Spanish Main.* Berkeley: University of California Press.

————. 1971. *Sixteenth Century North America.* Berkeley: University of California Press.

Schieffelin, Edward L. 1976. *The Sorrow of the Lonely and the Burning of the Dancers.* New York: St. Martin's Press.

Schmeck, Harold M. 1978. "First Worldwide Study of Fatal Virus Diseases Shows It Occurs in Mysterious Clusters." *New York Times,* July 31, p. A16.

Shankman, Paul. 1969. "Le Rôti et Le Boulli: Lévi-Strauss' Theory of Cannibalism." *American Anthropologist* 71:54–69.

Shapiro, Harry L. 1974. *Peking Man.* New York: Simon and Schuster.

Sheldon, William. 1820. "Brief Account of the Caribs, Who Inhabited the Antilles." *Transactions and Collections of the American Antiquarian Society* 1:366–433. Worcester, Mass.: William Manning.

Slutsky, Yehuda. 1971. "Blood Libel." In *Encyclopedia Judaica,* ed. Cecil Roth. Jerusalem: Keter Publishing House.

Soustelle, Jacques. 1962. *The Daily Life of the Aztecs,* trans. Patrick O'Brien. New York: The Macmillan Co.

Staden, Hans. 1929. *Hans Staden: The True Story of His Captivity 1557,* trans. Malcom Letts. New York: Robert M. McBride & Co.

Stanley, Henry M. 1878. *Through the Dark Continent.* New York: Harper and Brothers.

Steadman, Lyle. 1975. "Cannibal Witches among the Hewa." *Oceania* 46: 114–21.

Strabo. 1939. *The Geography of Strabo,* trans. and ed. H. L. Jones. Book 4. London: William Heinemann.

Strack, Herman L. 1909. *The Jew and Human Sacrifice.* New York: The Block Publishing Co.

Sullivan, Walter. 1976. "Both Laureates Found Major Clues in Studies of Primitive Tribesmen." *New York Times,* October 15, p. A13.

Tapia, Andrés de. 1963. The Chronicle of Andrés de Tapia. In *The Conquistadors,* ed. Patricia de Fuentes, pp. 17–48. New York: The Orion Press.

Teicher, Morton I. 1960. *Windigo Psychosis.* Seattle: American Ethnological Society.

Thevet, André. 1568. *The New Found World, or Antarctike.* London: Thomas Hackett.

Thwaites, Rueben G., ed. 1959. *The Jesuit Relations and Allied Documents.* Vol. 5. New York: Pageant Book Co.

Tremearne, A. J. N. 1912. *The Tailed Head-Hunters of Nigeria.* Philadelphia: J. B. Lippincott Co.

Trevor-Roper, H. R. 1969. *The European Witch-Craze of the Sixteenth and Seventeenth Centuries and Other Essays.* New York: Harper & Row Publishers.

Tuck, James A. 1974. "The Iroquois Confederacy." In *New World Archaeology,* ed. E. B. W. Zubrow et al., pp. 190–200. San Francisco: W. H. Freeman and Co.

Vaillant, George C. 1965. *Aztecs of Mexico.* Baltimore: Penguin Books.

Ward, Herbert. 1890. *Five Years with the Congo Cannibals.* London: Chatto & Windus.

Washburn, S. L. 1957. "Australopithecines: The Hunters or the Hunted." *American Anthropologist* 59:612–14.

Weeks, J. H. 1913. *Among Congo Cannibals.* Philadelphia: J. B. Lippincott Co.

Weidenreich, Franz. 1943. *The Skull of Sinanthropus Pekinensis.* Pehpei: Geological Survey of China.

Williams, G., et al. 1964. "An Evaluation of the Kuru Genetic Hypothesis." *Journal de Génétique Humaine* 13:11–21.

Wilson, Edward O. 1975. *Sociobiology.* Cambridge, Mass.: Harvard University Press.

Winter, E. H. 1959. *Beyond the Mountains of the Moon.* Urbana: The University of Illinois Press.

———. 1963. "The Enemy Within." In *Witchcraft and Sorcery in East Africa,* eds. John Middleton and E. H. Winter, pp. 277–99. London: Routledge and Kegan Paul.

Zegwaard, Rev. Gerald A. 1968. "Headhunting Practices of the Asmat of Netherlands New Guinea." In *Peoples and Cultures of the Pacific,* ed. Andrew P. Vayda, pp. 421–50. Garden City, N.Y.: The Natural History Press.

Zigas, V., and Gajdusek, D. C. 1957. "Kuru: Clinical Study of a New Syndrome Resembling Paralysis Agitans in Natives of the Eastern Highlands of Australian New Guinea." *The Medical Journal of Australia* 2:745–54.

———. 1959. "Kuru." *Papua and New Guinea Medical Journal* 3:1–24.

INDEX